MONETARY POLICY AT THE CUTTING EDGE

MONETARY POLICY AT THE CUTTING EDGE

SARAH R. PORTER
EDITOR

Nova Science Publishers, Inc.
New York

For permission to use material from this book please contact us:
Telephone 631-231-7269; Fax 631-231-8175
Web Site: http://www.novapublishers.com

Library of Congress Cataloging-in-Publication Data
Available upon request
ISBN: 978-1-60692-321-4

Published by Nova Science Publishers, Inc. ✢ New York

CONTENTS

PREFACE

Monetary policy can be defined as any policy relating to the supply of money. Since the agency concerned with the supply of money is the nation's central bank, the Federal Reserve, monetary policy can also be defined in terms of the directives, policies, statements, and actions of the Federal Reserve, particularly those from its Board of Governors that have an effect on national spending. The nation's financial press and markets pay particular attention to the pronouncements of the chairman of the Board of Governors, the nation's central banker. The reason for this attention is that monetary policy can have important effects on aggregate demand and through it on real Gross Domestic Product (GDP), unemployment, real foreign exchange rates, real interest rates, the composition of output, etc. It is paradoxical that these important effects, to the extent that they occur, are essentially only short run in nature. Over the longer run, the major effect of monetary policy is on the rate of inflation. Thus, while a more rapid rate of money growth may for a time stimulate the economy, leading to a more rapid rate of real GDP growth and a lower unemployment rate, over the longer run, these changes are undone and the economy is left with a higher rate of inflation. In some societies where high rates of inflation are endemic, more rapid rates of money growth fail to exercise any stimulating effect and are almost immediately translated into higher rates of inflation. Traditionally, two means have been used to measure the posture of monetary policy. Since monetary policy involves the Federal Reserve's contribution to aggregate demand or money spending, it would be logical to examine the growth rate of the money supply. A growing money supply is important for the subsequent growth in money spending or aggregate demand. Defining "the supply of money" has not been easy. For the United States, three different collections of assets have been defined as "money" and labeled M1, M2, and M3. Unfortunately, over the period 1990-2007, these aggregates have not been consistently linked to money spending and, consequently, they are not the major focus of monetary policy. Rather, the Federal Reserve executes monetary policy by setting a target for an overnight interest rate called the federal funds rate. Low or falling rates are usually taken as a sign of monetary ease; high or rising rates usually indicate monetary tightness. Changes in the federal funds rates affect primarily short-term interest rates, and through these changes, money spending.

Between January 3, 2001, and June 25, 2003, the target rate for federal funds was reduced to 1% from 6½%. This policy was reversed beginning June 30, 2004. In 17 equal increments ending on June 29, 2006, the target rate was raised to 5¼%. No additional changes were made until September 18, 2007 when, in a series of seven moves, the target was reduced to 2% on April 30. These reductions were designed to ease credit market conditions and stimulate spending.

Chapter 1 -It is paradoxical that these important effects, to the extent that they occur, are essentially only short run in nature. Over the longer run, the major effect of monetary policy is on the rate of inflation. Thus, while a more rapid rate of money growth may for a time stimulate the economy, leading to a more rapid rate of real GDP growth and a lower unemployment rate, over the longer run, these changes are undone and the economy is left with a higher rate of inflation. In some societies where high rates of inflation are endemic, more rapid rates of money growth fail to exercise any stimulating effect and are almost immediately translated into higher rates of inflation.

Traditionally, two means have been used to measure the posture of monetary policy. Since monetary policy involves the Federal Reserve's contribution to aggregate demand or money spending, it would be logical to examine the growth rate of the money supply. A growing money supply is important for the subsequent growth in money spending or aggregate demand. Defining "the supply of money" has not been easy. For the United States, three different collections of assets have been defined as "money" and labeled M1, M2, and M3. Unfortunately, over the period 1990-2007, these aggregates have not been consistently linked to money spending and, consequently, they are not the major focus of monetary policy.

Rather, the Federal Reserve executes monetary policy by setting a target for an overnight interest rate called the federal funds rate. Low or falling rates are usually taken as a sign of monetary ease; high or rising rates usually indicate monetary tightness. Changes in the federal funds rates affect primarily short-term interest rates, and through these changes, money spending.

Between January 3, 2001, and June 25, 2003, the target rate for federal funds was reduced to 1% from 61/2%. This policy was reversed beginning June 30, 2004.

In 17 equal increments ending on June 29, 2006, the target rate was raised to 51/4%. No additional changes were made until September 18, 2007 when, in a series of seven moves, the target was reduced to 2% on April 30. These reductions were designed to ease credit market conditions and stimulate spending.

Chapter 2 - Emerging market economies often face sudden stops in capital inflows or reduced access to the international capital market. This paper analyzes what monetary policy should accomplish in such an event. Optimal monetary policy induces higher interest rates and exchange rate depreciation. The interest rate hike discourages borrowing and consumption, mitigating the impact of the increased cost of borrowing. The exchange rate depreciation provides a boost to export revenues, reducing the need for, but not averting, a domestic recession. The paper shows that the arrival of the sudden stop further aggravates the time inconsistency problem. Optimal policy is fairly well approximated by a flexible targeting rule, which stabilizes a basket composed of domestic price inflation, exchange rate and output. We show that from a welfare perspective, the success of a fixed exchange rate regime depends on the economic environment. For the benchmark parameterization, the peg performs the worst of the simple rules considered. For alternative parameterizations that feature low nominal rigidities or high elasticity of foreign demand, the fixed exchange rate regime performs relatively better.

Chapter 3 - In recent years, financial commentators have linked stock market bubbles and housing price booms to excess liquidity in the financial system and an expansive monetary policy. However, in making these connections, the commentators often rely heavily on metaphors: "Holding interest rates too low for too long creates excess liquidity, which is now more likely to spill into the prices of homes, shares, or other assets." Or "the flood of global liquidity . . . has inflated a series of asset-price bubbles." While figurative statements of this kind may be rhetorically effective, they tend to be quite imprecise, providing little insight into the economic mecha nisms underlying the linkages they describe.

Chapter 4 - The dollar's value in international exchange has been falling since early 2002. Over this five year span, the currency, on a real trade weighted basis, is down about 29%. For most of this time the dollar's fall was moderately paced at about 3.0% to 4.0% annually. Recently, however, the slide has accelerated, falling nearly 10% between January and December of 2007. An acceleration of the depreciation brings the periodic concern of an impending dollar crisis to the fore. There is no precise demarcation of when a falling dollar moves from being an orderly decline to being a crisis. Most likely it would be a situation where the dollar falls, perhaps 15% to 20% annually for several years, and sends a significant negative shock to the U.S. and the global economies. This crisis may not be an inevitable outcome, but one that likely presents considerable risk to the economy.

The large U.S. current account deficits are sustained by an inflow of foreign capital. That inflow also exerts upward pressure on the value of the dollar as investors demand dollars to enable the purchase of dollar denominated assets. There is a limit to how much external debt even the U.S. economy can incur. Erasing the U.S. trade gap would stop the accumulation of debt. This would occur through a rebalancing of global spending, composed of a decrease of domestic spending in the United States and an increase of domestic spending in the surplus economies. Such shifts in domestic spending patterns must be induced by a depreciation of the dollar, causing the price of foreign goods to rise for U.S. buyers and the price of U.S. goods to fall for foreign buyers.

The critical factor governing whether orderly and disorderly adjustment of international imbalances occurs is foreign investor expectations about future dollar depreciation. Rational expectations will have a smoothing effect on the size of international capital flows. In contrast, a sharp plunge of the dollar is likely to occur if investors do not form rational expectations. If the dollar then depreciates at a rate faster than foreign investors now expect, a dollar crisis becomes likely. Currently foreign investors do not appear to have a realistic expectation of future dollar depreciation. A dollar crisis could start when they realize their error and try to move quickly out of dollar assets — the likely stampede would cause a "dollar crisis." Three prominent counter-arguments to the dollar crisis prediction (the *global savings glut* argument, the *Bretton Woods II* argument, and the *economic dark matter* argument) do not offer credible alternatives to the dollar crisis outcome.

The transition to a new equilibrium of trade balances may not be smooth, likely involving a slowdown in economic activity or a recession. The ongoing U.S. housing price crisis raises the risk of a dollar crisis causing a recession. With fiscal policy most likely out of consideration in the near term, the task of attempting to counter the short-term contractionary effects of a dollar crisis would fall upon the Federal Reserve. A stimulative monetary policy can be implemented quickly but its eventual effectiveness is uncertain. The most useful policy response by foreign economies would be complementary expansionary policies to offset the negative impact of their appreciating currencies on their net exports. Attempts to defend a currency against this crisis driven appreciation would be costly and likely fail.

Chapter 5 - In 1913, Congress created the Federal Reserve System to serve as the central bank for the United States. The Federal Reserve formulates the nation's monetary policy, supervises and regulates banks, and provides a variety of financial services to depository financial institutions and the federal government. The System comprises three major components, the Board of Governors, a network of 12 Federal Reserve Banks, and member banks.

Congress created the Federal Reserve as an independent agency to enable the central bank to carry out its responsibilities protected from excessive political and private pressures. At the same time, by law and practice, the Federal Reserve is accountable to Congress. The seven members of the board are appointed by the President with the advice and consent of the Senate. Congress routinely monitors the Federal Reserve System through formal and informal oversight activities. This chapter examines the structure and operations of the major components of the Federal Reserve System, and provides an overview of congressional oversight activities.

In: Monetary Policy at the Cutting Edge
Editor: Sarah R. Porter, pp. 1-20
ISBN: 978-1-60692-321-4

Chapter 1

MONETARY POLICY AND THE FEDERAL RESERVE: CURRENT POLICY AND CONDITIONS*

***Marc Labonte*[1] *and Gail E. Makinen*[2]**

ABSTRACT

Monetary policy can be defined as any policy relating to the supply of money. Since the agency concerned with the supply of money is the nation's central bank, the Federal Reserve, monetary policy can also be defined in terms of the directives, policies, statements, and actions of the Federal Reserve, particularly those from its Board of Governors that have an effect on national spending. The nation's financial press and markets pay particular attention to the pronouncements of the chairman of the Board of Governors, the nation's central banker. The reason for this attention is that monetary policy can have important effects on aggregate demand and through it on real Gross Domestic Product (GDP), unemployment, real foreign exchange rates, real interest rates, the composition of output, etc.

It is paradoxical that these important effects, to the extent that they occur, are essentially only short run in nature. Over the longer run, the major effect of monetary policy is on the rate of inflation. Thus, while a more rapid rate of money growth may for a time stimulate the economy, leading to a more rapid rate of real GDP growth and a lower unemployment rate, over the longer run, these changes are undone and the economy is left with a higher rate of

---

* Excerpted from CRS Report RL30354, dated April 30, 2008.

inflation. In some societies where high rates of inflation are endemic, more rapid rates of money growth fail to exercise any stimulating effect and are almost immediately translated into higher rates of inflation.

Traditionally, two means have been used to measure the posture of monetary policy. Since monetary policy involves the Federal Reserve's contribution to aggregate demand or money spending, it would be logical to examine the growth rate of the money supply. A growing money supply is important for the subsequent growth in money spending or aggregate demand. Defining "the supply of money" has not been easy. For the United States, three different collections of assets have been defined as "money" and labeled M1, M2, and M3. Unfortunately, over the period 1990-2007, these aggregates have not been consistently linked to money spending and, consequently, they are not the major focus of monetary policy.

Rather, the Federal Reserve executes monetary policy by setting a target for an overnight interest rate called the federal funds rate. Low or falling rates are usually taken as a sign of monetary ease; high or rising rates usually indicate monetary tightness. Changes in the federal funds rates affect primarily short-term interest rates, and through these changes, money spending.

Between January 3, 2001, and June 25, 2003, the target rate for federal funds was reduced to 1% from 61/2%. This policy was reversed beginning June 30, 2004. In 17 equal increments ending on June 29, 2006, the target rate was raised to 51/4%. No additional changes were made until September 18, 2007 when, in a series of seven moves, the target was reduced to 2% on April 30. These reductions were designed to ease credit market conditions and stimulate spending.

INTRODUCTION

The behavior of the U.S. economy is affected significantly by the behavior of monetary policy. And monetary policy over the past three years has been supportive of a continued and sustained economic expansion. Monetary policy changes typically affect the economy with a 12- to 18-month lag.

The 1991-2001 economic expansion, the longest in American history, came to an end in March 2001. Economic growth became sluggish during the second half of 2000 and remained sluggish through 2001. During that year, GDP contracted during the first and third quarters. Growth resumed in the fourth quarter and has continued through the end of 2007 (for which data are now available). Prior to mid-2000, the economy was growing at a rate that was thought to be unsustainable. To curb growth, the Federal Reserve between mid-1999 and May 2000 raised the target for the federal funds rate to 61/2% from 43/4%. This tightening was too severe, for economic growth slumped, industrial production declined and unemployment rose.

The Federal Reserve then began aggressively easing monetary policy. Between January 3, 2001, and June 25, 2003, the target for the federal funds rate was reduced to 1% from 61/2%. Short-term interest rates generally followed the decline in the target for the federal funds rate, whereas longer-term rates proven more resilient and did fall as much. As the economy recovered and expanded, monetary policy was gradually tightened. In 17 moves between June 30, 2004, and June 29, 2006, the target was increased to 51/4%. No changes were made until September 18, 2007, when target reduction began. In seven moves ending on April 30, 2008, the target was reduced to 2%. This was designed to ease pressures in financial markets and stimulate spending.

The growth rates of the various measures of money have been quite different and do not always provide information on the shifts in monetary policy. The only measure that has enjoyed a fairly consistent rate of growth is the monetary base that is composed largely of circulating paper currency, much of which appears to be abroad and is not necessarily related to economic conditions in the United States.

WHAT IS MONETARY POLICY?

Broadly speaking, monetary policy is any policy related to the supply of money. As such, it would encompass various activities of the U.S. Treasury for those relating to foreign exchange operations and the receipt and disposition of public funds can affect the supply of money. The dominant influence on the U.S. money supply, however, comes from the policies of the nation's central bank, the Federal Reserve, and particularly those policies originating with its Board of Governors.[1] Thus, a more realistic definition of monetary policy would be that it consists of the directives, policies, pronouncements, and actions of the Federal Reserve that affect aggregate demand or national spending. Among these, the dominant action consists of open market operations. These involve the buying and selling of seasoned Treasury securities by the Federal Reserve. When Treasury securities are purchased, the Federal Reserve does so with newly created money. This money can serve as reserves for the financial system and allows commercial banks and other depository institutions to make new loans and investments, thereby expanding the money supply and aggregate demand. The opposite happens when the Federal Reserve sells government securities.

Is Monetary Policy Important?

It has been said that "money matters" and the case for this statement can be made in at least two different contexts. In one, monetary policy is compared with fiscal policy and, given the current international financial system with flexible exchange rates and a high degree of capital mobility between countries, the ability of changes in the money supply to affect aggregate demand and the pace of GDP growth and employment is great compared with fiscal policy. In the other context, changes in the money supply have the potential to bring about major changes in the growth of GDP and employment only in the *short run.* Paradoxically, this is not true over the *longer run.* Over the more extended horizon, money supply growth has its primary effect only on the rate of inflation. How fast GDP grows or what the unemployment rate is, is largely independent of the amount of money or its growth rate. A brief discussion of each of the two contexts summarized above follows.

Monetary vs. Fiscal Policy

The standard macroeconomic model makes a compelling case for the relative importance of monetary policy in a world whose financial arrangements involve the use of flexible exchange rates and where capital is highly mobile between countries. To see this, fiscal and monetary expansion will be contrasted.

Let us allow the full employment budget deficit to rise (or the full-employment surplus to fall) through either a tax rate cut or a rise in appropriated expenditures. While the increase in this budget deficit (or fall in surplus) raises aggregate demand, it also raises the borrowing requirement of the government (or lowers the amount of debt it retires) and its demand for funds in financial markets. This then causes domestic interest rates to rise relative to those in other financial centers. The rise in domestic interest rates makes U.S. financial assets more attractive to foreigners. They, in turn, increase the demand for dollars in foreign exchange markets to acquire the wherewithal to purchase U.S. assets. The increased demand for dollars causes the dollar to appreciate. Dollar appreciation then reduces the cost of foreign goods and services to Americans and raises the price of American goods and services to foreigners. As a result, U.S. spending on imports tends to rise and foreign spending on U.S. exports tends to fall. Thus, any expansionary effects on domestic demand from the larger budget deficit tends to be offset in part or total by a reduced foreign trade surplus or a larger foreign trade deficit.[2]

A more expansive monetary policy centering on a more rapid rate of growth of the money supply initially serves to lower U.S. interest rates relative to those in other financial centers. Foreign financial assets become more attractive to U.S.

investors, the supply of dollars to the foreign exchange markets rises as U.S. investors attempt to acquire foreign currencies to buy foreign assets, and the dollar depreciates. Dollar depreciation then makes foreign goods and services more expensive to Americans and American goods and services cheaper to foreigners. As a result, the United States spends less on imports and foreigners spend more on U.S. exports. A falling foreign trade deficit or rising trade surplus thus reinforces any stimulus to domestic demand that comes from lower U.S. interest rates.

The implication from the standard macroeconomic model is that monetary expansion is far more powerful than fiscal policy in influencing GDP growth and employment.

Short Run vs. Longer Run

The analysis above quite clearly shows that a more rapid rate of growth of the money supply can cause domestic demand to expand. An examination of U.S. economic history will show that money-induced demand expansions can have a positive effect on U.S. GDP growth and total employment. This same evidence, however, also suggests that over the longer run, a more rapid rate of growth of the money supply is largely dissipated in a more rapid rate of inflation with little if any lasting effect on real GDP and employment.

Economists have two explanations for this paradoxical behavior. First, they note that, in the short run, many economies have an elaborate system of contracts (both implicit and explicit) that makes it difficult in a short period for significant adjustments to take place in wages and prices in response to more rapid money growth. Second, they note that expectations for one reason or another are slow to adjust to the longer run consequences of major changes in monetary policy. This slow adjustment also adds rigidities to wages and prices. Because of these rigidities, changes in money supply growth that change aggregate demand can have a large initial effect on output and employment. Over the longer run, as contracts are renegotiated and expectations adjust, wages and prices rise in response to the change in demand and much of the change in output and employment is undone. Thus, money can matter in the short run but be fairly neutral for GDP growth and employment in the longer run.

It is noteworthy that in societies where high rates of inflation are endemic, the short run may be very short indeed. During the final stages of very rapid inflations, called hyperinflation, money's ability to alter GDP growth and employment is virtually nonexistent.

INDICATORS OF MONETARY POLICY

It is common to speak of monetary policy as being "easy" or being "tight" or even of being "neutral." What exactly do these terms mean and how does one measure the posture of monetary policy?

Two basic measures of the posture of monetary policy are frequently used: the growth rate of the money supply and market interest rates, particularly the federal funds rate (the interest rate that one bank charges another for reserves that are lent on an overnight basis). Unfortunately, as the following discussion makes clear, neither of these two indicators provides an unambiguous measure of the posture of monetary policy.

Money Supply Growth

Because the growth in aggregate demand depends heavily on the growth in the supply of money, it would be logical to measure the posture of monetary policy by the growth rate of the supply of money. Using this indicator, monetary policy is said to be *easy* when, during a sustained period, the supply of money increases at a rate that is high or rising relative to a recent trend. Alternatively, policy is said to be *tight* when the rate of money growth is low or falling relative to a trend.

To measure the posture of monetary policy, the abstract concept "the supply of money" must be given an empirical content. That is, the supply of money must be defined in terms of an asset or group of assets that can be measured. Moreover, that asset or group of assets must be stably or predictably related to aggregate demand or money spending. The latter condition is important. It means that, when the supply of money is changed, it will be possible to predict its effect on money spending.

The United States does not have a unique asset or group of assets that the Federal Reserve defines as money. Rather, three collections of assets have been recognized as money and are designated as M1, M2, and M3 (for a definition of each, see the appendix).[3] They are constructed such that M3 includes M2, and M2 includes M1. It is possible for the growth of one or two of the aggregates to rise or fall when the growth of the other aggregate or aggregates falls or rises (a common reason for this is that wealth owners can shift dollars from one type of account to another such as when they shift from passbook savings, an account included in M2 but not M1, into checking accounts on which interest is paid, an account included in both M1 and M2). When these divergent movements take place, as they frequently have during the past 12 years in the United States (see Table 2), it is difficult to characterized monetary policy.

A simple way to answer this question is to see which aggregate best explains the subsequent movements in aggregate demand. During much of the post-World War II period, M1 had the most stable relationship to aggregate demand. Nevertheless, the Federal Reserve, beginning in the 1 970s, set target growth rate ranges for all three aggregates. Unfortunately, during the late 1970s, the stable relationship between M1 and aggregate spending broke down and the Federal Reserve, while still reporting movements in this aggregate, no longer sets growth rate ranges for it. During the 1990s, the stable relationship between M2 and aggregate spending also broke down. Beginning in July 2000, the Fed discontinued setting monitoring ranges for M2 and M3. Legislation requiring it to do so expired. (Although M3 was never strongly related to aggregate demand, its movement bore little relationship to subsequent movements in demand during the 1990s and it was discontinued in 2006).

Thus, the United States has had three definitions of money that appear to provide little information about the posture of monetary policy. Moreover, an extensive amount of recent research on the stability issue has yet to yield a collection of new assets that performs consistently better, that is, provide consistently superior information on the posture of monetary policy.[4]

Interest Rates

A logical reason for focusing on interest rates in judging monetary policy is that they are an important link by which changes in the money supply are transmitted to the real economy. That is, changes in money supply growth lead to changes in market interest rates and these changes then influence households in their decisions to buy homes, automobiles, appliances, and the like, and businesses in their decisions regarding inventories and plant and equipment purchases.

The interest rate relevant for these decisions is not the market rate but the real rate or market rate less the expected rate of inflation. Rising real rates are interpreted as a sign of tight monetary policy while falling real rates supposedly signal a move toward an easier monetary policy. Caution should be used, however, in making this interpretation of the movement in real rates. The reason is that market interest rates respond both to shifts in the supply and demand for money.[5]

Those who use interest rates as guides to the posture of monetary policy appear to implicitly assume that shifts in the supply of money dominate movements in the relevant interest rates. Thus, a more rapid rate of growth of the money supply should drive down market interest rates, especially short-term rates. Given expectations about future inflation, the fall in market rates is taken as a fall in real rates and a signal that monetary policy has eased; and, conversely, for a rise in market and real rates.

Market interest rates, however, can fall for two other reasons even when the supply of money (or its growth rate) is held constant. First, any fall in income reduces the demand for money and, as a result, market interest rates and real rates will fall. Second, should the public come to expect a lower inflation rate, inflation expectations should also fall. With this decline, market interest rates should also fall. However, real interest rates should not fall and may even rise in the short run. Thus, the fall in market rates should not stimulate economic activity.

An important interest rate for the Federal Reserve is the federal funds rate, which is essentially an overnight rate that one depository institution charges another when reserves are lent — reserves being necessary to back the deposit liabilities financial institutions have on their books. If the Federal Reserve wishes to expand the reserves of depository institutions thereby enhancing their lending capabilities, it will supply reserves to this market. The increased supply will drive down the federal funds rate and monetary policy can be said to have eased.

Conversely, when the Federal Reserve wishes to tighten lending, it will withdraw reserves from this market causing the funds rate to rise. Thus, a falling funds rate is often taken to signal an easing of monetary policy, a rising rate the tightening of policy, and a constant rate, a neutral or "stand fast" policy. However, this is not always the case and each movement can have unintended consequences.

This arises because the Federal Reserve, through the federal funds rate, only controls the supply of reserves. It does not control the demand for reserves. That is in the domain of financial institutions and is governed by their outlook for economic activity. A constant federal funds rate, for example, may not be a neutral policy. Suppose that financial institutions become pessimistic about the future and cut back their demand for reserves. Reserve growth declines as does lending and economic activity. During the period these advents are transpiring, the Federal Reserve keeps the funds rate constant. The effect on the economy is not neutral.

How long this would continue before it became apparent to the Federal Reserve that the economy had shifted is open to conjecture. After some period of time, data would reveal the falloff in the growth of the reserves of depository institutions and the monetary aggregates. Misinterpretations such as this are most costly when an economy is at a critical turning point.

THE RECENT AND CURRENT POSTURE OF MONETARY POLICY

The behavior of several important performance characteristics of the U.S. economy since the early 1980s is shown in Table 1. One period of interest is GDP growth from 1994 to 2000. At that time, growth rates of from 4% to 5% were regarded as unsustainable. These rates likely played an important role in causing the Federal Reserve to tighten monetary policy. And this tightening played an important role in bringing to an end the longest economic expansion in U.S. history (March 1991 to March 2000), as well as setting in motion the current expansion. As noted above, there are two ways to measure the posture of monetary policy: the growth of the monetary aggregates and interest rates.

The behavior of the aggregates is shown in Table 2. The first impression is that they do not tell a consistent story. Aggregate Reserves and to a lesser degree M1 contracted during most of 1994-2002, whereas the Monetary Base, M2, and M3 grew positively in each year (a definition of each aggregate is given in the appendix). All is, however, not what it seems. The decline in Aggregate Reserves actually allowed for considerable monetary expansion. This occurs because individuals and businesses allowed their demand deposit balances to run off (see Table 3). This decline in demand deposit balances has set free bank reserves. Since not all of these reserves were removed from the banking system, reserve contraction is compatible with expanding the lending capacity of banks. (The increase in aggregate reserves in 2001 was temporary and designed to forestall a possible liquidity crisis in the immediate aftermath of the September 11 terrorist attacks.) The shift to positive reserve growth during 2003 and 2004 reflects the fall in the federal funds target during those years. The contraction of reserves during 2005 and 2006 reflects the increase in the target for federal funds that began in mid-2004.

The behavior of the Monetary Base could account for both the recovery that began in the fourth quarter of 2001 and the subsequent expansion of the economy. However, this may be due to chance since approximately 90% of the Base consists of paper currency (and coin) in circulation, much of which apparently does not circulate within the United States.[6] Thus, its behavior may depend on conditions in foreign countries rather than reflect economic developments in the United States.

Table 1. Recent Economic Performance

Year	Real Growth[a]	Inflation Rate[b]	Unemployment Rate
1983	7.7	3.4	9.6
1984	5.6	3.6	7.5
1985	4.2	2.8	7.2
1986	2.8	2.4	7.0
1987	4.5	2.8	6.2
1988	3.7	3.8	5.5
1989	2.7	3.4	5.3
1990	0.7	4.1	5.6
1991	1.1	3.0	6.8
1992	4.1	2.2	7.5
1993	2.5	2.3	6.9
1994	4.1	2.2	6.1[c]
1995	2.0	2.0	5.6
1996	4.4	1.9	5.4
1997	4.3	1.5	4.9
1998	4.5	1.1	4.5
1999	4.7	1.6	4.2
2000	2.3	2.2	4.0
2001	0.2	2.5	4.7
2002	1.9	1.7	5.8
2003	3.7	2.1	6.0
2004	3.1	3.2	5.5
2005	2.9	3.4	5.1
2006	2.6	2.7	4.6
2007	2.5	2.6	4.6

Source: U.S. Departments of Labor and Commerce.

[a] Real growth and inflation are measured on a fourth quarter over fourth quarter basis.

[b] Inflation is measured by the implicit price deflator for GDP on a fourth quarter over fourth quarter basis.

[c] The unemployment rates subsequent to 1994 are not strictly comparable with those of previous years. Annual averages for all years.

Alternatively, the behavior of all three Ms could account for the beginning of the expansion and its continuation. However, M1's behavior in 2005 does not bode well for a continuation of the expansion. This is not mirrored in the behavior of M3.

A general conclusion from the behavior of the aggregates is that, while they might yield some useful information about the economic expansion, they do not provide consistent information on the posture of monetary policy since it is well known that they are not used by the Federal Reserve to manipulate the growth in aggregate demand. Rather, the behavior of the Federal Reserve and the posture of monetary policy is best inferred from interest rates, particularly the behavior of the federal funds rate.

The movement of selected U.S. Treasury yields and the federal funds rate is shown in Figure 1. The sharp decline in the rate that began in late 1990 played a major role in initiating the record cyclical upswing that began in March 1991. As the expansion began to take hold, the Federal Reserve kept the rate target constant at about 3% from late 1992 through early 1994. As momentum built and the economy moved toward full employment, the rate was raised to slow growth. The increase appeared to be too large as GDP growth slowed to about 2.3% in 1995. In three small adjustments, the last on January 31, 1996, the federal funds rate target was lowered to 51/4%. The growth rate of GDP during 1996 was above the rate the Federal Reserve thought to be sustainable. As a result, the federal funds rate target was hiked to 51/2% on March 25, 1997. However, beginning in the second quarter of 1998, GDP growth slowed. To boost demand and provide support to ease the Asian and Russian financial crises, the target was reduced by 1/4% on September 29, October 15, and November 17, 1998. As the crisis eased, the rate target was hiked by 1/4% in June, August, and November of 1999. To slow GDP growth to a sustainable rate, the target was hiked on February 2, March 21, and May 16, 2000, bringing it to 61/2%. It appears that these increases had too severe an effect on GDP growth, for the target was reduced to 6% on January 3, 2001. Between then and August 21, the rate was reduced in six moves to 31/2%. On September 17, to avert a liquidity crisis following the terrorist attacks of 9/11, the rate was reduced to 3%. In a follow-up action, it was reduced three more times and on December 11, it stood at 13/4%. The target rate was reduced once in 2002 (November 6) and once in 2003 (June 25) to a low of 1%. As the growth rate accelerated, the unemployment rate fell, and the inflation rate showed signs of strengthening, the Fed tightened policy. Between June 30, 2004, and June 29, 2006, the target was increased 17 times and then stood at 51/4%. On September 18, October 31, and December 11, 2007, and January 22 and 30, March 18, and April 30, 2008, was reduced incrementally to 2% to provide liquidity to financial markets and to stimulate spending.

Note that, while short-term interest rates move in sympathy with the federal funds rate, longer-term rates often do not. The divergence is especially noticeable during 1996, 1997, 1999, and 2001 to 2007. This should help dispel the notion that the Federal Reserve can set interest rates wherever it wishes.

Table 2. The Growth Rates of the Monetary Aggregates (annual rate of change)

Time Period	Aggregate Reserves	Monetary Base	M1	M2	M3[a]
91:12-92:12	19.6	10.5	14.3	1.6	0.3
92:12-93:12	11.3	10.5	10.3	1.6	1.4
93:12-94:12	1.8	8.2	1.8	0.4	1.7
94:12-95:12	5.0	3.9	2.0	4.1	6.0
95:12-96:12	-11.2	4.0	4.1	4.7	7.3
96:12-97:12	6.6	6.1	0.7	5.7	9.1
97:12-98:12	-3.5	7.0	2.2	8.8	11.0
98:12-99:12	-7.6	15.3	2.3	6.0	8.3
99:12-00:12	-7.3	-1.5	-3.0	6.2	8.6
00:12-01:12	6.7	8.7	8.3	10.5	12.9
01:12-02:12	-2.8	7.2	3.2	6.4	6.5
02:12-03:12	6.9	5.7	6.2	4.6	3.3
03:12-04:12	8.8	5.4	5.2	5.7	6.4
04:12-05:12	-4.3	3.6	0.0	4.1	7.8
05:12-06:12	-4-4	3.1	-0.5	5.3	NA
06:12-07:12	-1.7	1.4	0.0	5.9	NA
07:03-08:03	4.3	1.5	0.2	7.0	NA

Source: Board of Governors of the Federal Reserve System. a. Data on M3 ceased to be published in March 2006.

[a]. Data on M3 ceased to be published in March 2006.

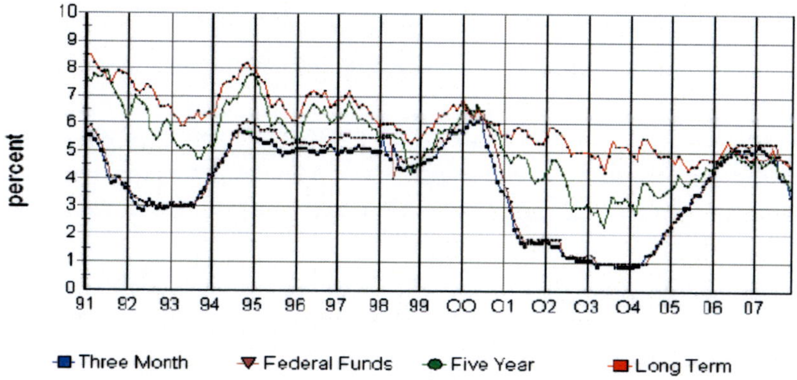

Source: Board of Governors of the Federal Reserve System.

Figure 1. Yield on Selected Securities and Federal Funds.

Table 3. Growth in Major Components of M2 (annualized rates of change)

Time Period	Currency	Demand Deposits	Other Checking Deposits	Nontransactions Component[a]
92:12-93:12	10.1	13.4	7.9	-2.1
93:12-94:12	10.0	-0.5	-2.5	-0.2
94:12-95:12	5.1	1.5	-11.8	7.1
95:12-96:12	5.9	3.4	-22.6	8.7
96:12-97:12	7.7	-1.7	!11.0	8.2
97:12-98:12	8.2	-4.1	1.8	11.2
98:12-99:12	12.2	-6.2	-2.5	6.9
99:12-01:12	2.4	-11.9	-1.6	9.2
00:12-01:12	9.5	6.3	8.4	11.2
01:12-02:12	7.8	-9.0	8.2	7.5
02:12-03:12	5.8	3.5	11.2	4.1
03:12-04:12	5.3	5.5	5.6	5.6
04:12-05:12	3.7	-4.6	-3.4	5.2
05:12-06:12	3.5	-5.6	-4.5	6.8
06:12-07:12	1.3	-4.3	0.4	7.3
07:03-08:03	1.2	-2.5	0.5	8.6

Source: Board of Governors of the Federal Reserve System.

THE FEDERAL RESERVE AND THE MONETARY AGGREGATES

In its report to Congress, dated July 20, 1993, the Board of Governors expressed considerable uncertainty about the usefulness of M2 and M3 as measures of money. The uncertainty arose from the perverse movement in the velocity or turnover rates of these aggregates during the previous three years.

For this reason, the Board of Governors decided to de-emphasize both M2 and M3 in its decision-making. While the board continued to set growth rate ranges for each aggregate, it concluded:

> With considerable uncertainty persisting about the relationship of the monetary aggregates to spending, the behavior of the aggregates relative to their annual ranges will likely be of limited use in guiding policy ... and the Federal Reserve will continue to utilize a broad range of financial and economic indicators in assessing its policy stance.

This position was reaffirmed by the board during subsequent Monetary Policy (formerly called Humphrey-Hawkins) hearings. However, in the Monetary Policy Report submitted to Congress on July 20, 2000, the Board of Governors stated:

> At its June meeting, the FOMC did not establish ranges for the growth of money and debt in 2000 and 2001. The legal requirement to establish and to announce such ranges had expired, and owing to uncertainties about the behavior of the velocities of debt and money, these ranges for many years have not provided useful benchmarks for the conduct of monetary policy. Nevertheless, the FOMC believes that the behavior of money and credit will continue to have value for gauging economic and financial conditions....

Even this view of the usefulness of the aggregates has changed. The Board of Governors announced in November 2005 that beginning in March 23, 2006, it would no longer publish data on M3. In the words of the Board: "... publication of M3 was judged to be no longer generating sufficient benefit in the analysis of the economy or of the financial sector to justify the costs of publication."[7]

The Federal Reserve and the Discount Rate

The Federal Reserve has preferred to conduct monetary policy by setting a target for the federal funds rate. This method has allowed the Federal Reserve to adopt an activist posture in the conduct of monetary policy. The Board of Governors controls another interest rate, the discount rate. Financial institutions can borrow on a temporary basis directly from the Federal Reserve at this rate. The Board can either grant or deny the loan. The initiation of the loan, however, is at the discretion of the borrowing financial institution. In this sense, the Federal Reserve is passive in the process. Although the discount rate has long been a tool of central banking, it has fallen into disuse in the United States over the past several decades. Financial institutions prefer to borrow overnight in the federal funds market because they can obtain what they need without having to subject their borrowing needs to the purview of the Federal Reserve. On the downside, borrowing federal funds is generally on an overnight basis where as borrowing at the discount window is for a longer period. In conducting monetary policy, the Board has, in the past, moved the discount rate in sympathy with the federal funds target. For much of the past decade, the discount rate was set slightly below the federal funds target.

To discourage financial institutions from borrowing at the discount window, lending rules were altered in early 2003. Since that time, the discount rate has been set above the federal funds rate target and is now a penalty rate. However, a change in the discount rate independent from a change in the federal funds target can send a powerful message to financial markets. For example, on August 17, 2007, the Board of Governors, concerned about the adequacy of liquidity in national financial markets, reduced the discount rate for primary credit to 43/4% from 51/4%. Later, on September 18, October 31, December 11, 2007, January 22 and 30, March 18, and April 30, 2008, when the federal funds target was reduced, the discount rate was also reduced replicating past behavior by the Federal Reserve (in addition, on March16, 2008, the discount rate was lowered without any change in the federal funds target).

The Federal Reserve's Mandate and Its Independence

The Constitution grants Congress the power to "coin money, and regulate the value thereof...." However, operational responsibility for making U.S. monetary policy has been delegated by Congress to the Fed. Congress is still responsible for oversight, setting the Fed's mandate and approving the President's nominations for the Fed's Board of Governors, but several institutional features grant it significant "independence" from the political process.[8] The Federal Reserve system is quasi-public in structure: it is owned by its member banks. The governors are appointed to staggered 14-year terms, and can only be removed by Congress for cause. It is self-funded and does not receive appropriations. While it must follow its congressional mandate, it has been granted broad *discretion* to interpret and carry out that mandate as it sees fit on a day-to-day basis. Most economists argue that good monetary policy depends on independence because it reduces the temptation to raise inflation in the long run in order to lower unemployment in the short run. Researchers have made cross-country comparisons to try to make the case that countries with independent central banks are more likely to have low inflation rates and better economic performance.[9]

As a practical matter, the Fed's mandate can be seen as a further source of political independence. The Federal Reserve Act of 1977 (P.L. 95-188, 91 Stat. 1387) charged the Fed with "the goals of maximum employment, stable prices, and moderate long-term interest rates." Note that the Fed controls none of these three indicators directly; it controls only overnight interest rates. Because it has only one tool at its disposal and three goals, there will be times when the goals will be at odds with each other, and the Fed will have to choose to pursue one at the expense of the other two. Critics have argued that the ambiguity inherent in the current mandate makes for less than optimal transparency and accountability. It may also strengthen political independence if it allows the Fed to deflect congressional criticism by pointing, at any given time, to whatever goal justifies its current policy stance.

The most popular alternative to the current mandate is to replace it with a single mandate of price stability. Under this proposal, the Fed would typically be given (or, under the version mooted by Chairman Bernanke, give itself) a numerical inflation target, and would then be required to set monetary policy with the goal of meeting the target on an ongoing basis.[10] Proponents of inflation targeting say that maximum employment and moderate interest rates are not meaningful policy goals because monetary policy has no long-term influence over either one. They argue a mandate that focused on keeping inflation low would deliver better economic results and improve transparency and oversight. Opponents, including former Chairman Greenspan, say that the flexibility inherent in the current system has served the United States well in the past 25 years, delivering both low inflation and economic stability, and there is little reason to fix a system that is not broken. They argue that some focus on employment is appropriate given that monetary policy has powerful short-term effects on it, and that too great a focus on inflation could lead to a overly volatile business cycle. Inflation targeting has been widely adopted abroad, although foreign inflation targeters seem to target inflation less strictly in practice than some of its proponents may have hoped.[11]

Congressional Oversight and The Near-Term Goals of Monetary Policy

The primary form of congressional oversight of the Federal Reserve are the semi-annual hearings with the Senate Committee on Banking, Housing, and Urban Affairs and the House Committee on Financial Services. At these hearings, which take place in February and July, the Fed Chairman presents the Fed's *Monetary Policy Report to the Congress*, testifies, and responds to questions from committee members. These hearings and reporting requirements were established by the Full Employment Act of 1978 (P.L. 95-523, 92 Stat 1897), also known as the Humphrey-Hawkins Act, and renewed in the American Homeownership and Economic Opportunity Act of 2000 (P.L. 106-569).

The Monetary Policy Report presents a review of recent economic and monetary policy developments, as well as economic projections for 2008 through 2010. Since monetary policy plays an important role in determining economic outcomes, these projections can be viewed as the Fed's perceptions of how today's monetary policy stance will influence future economic conditions. The most recent projections from the February 27, 2008 *Monetary Policy Report*, representing the views of the Board of Governors and the 12 Reserve Bank Presidents are presented in Table 4. These are contrasted with the projections made for similar variables by the Federal Reserve last October.[12]

Table 4. Federal Reserve System Economic Projections (percent)

	2008	2009	2010
Growth of real GDP	1.3 to 2.0	2.1 to 2.7	2.5 to 3.0
October Projections	*1.8 to 2.5*	*2.3 to 2.7*	*2.5 to 2.6*
Unemployment Rate	5.2 to 5.3	5.0 to 5.3	4.9 to 5.1
October Projections	*4.8 to 4.9*	*4.8 to 4.9*	*4.7 to 4.9*
PCE inflation[a]	2.1 to 2.4	1.7 to 2.0	1.7 to 2.0
October Projections	*1.8 to 2.1*	*1.7 to 2.0*	*1.6 to 1.9*

Table 4. (Continued).

	2008	2009	2010
Core PCE inflation	2.0 to 2.2	1.7 to 2.0	1.7 to 1.9
October Projections	*1.7 to 1.9*	*1.7 to 1.9*	*1.6 to 1.9*

Source: Table complied by CRS from the February 27, 2008 *Monetary Policy Report.*

[a]. These projections use the price index for Personal Consumption Expenditures obtained from the Gross Domestic Product accounts. The Core PCE is the PCE less food and energy.

APPENDIX. DEFINITIONS

M1 is the sum of the following:

1 Currency held by the public
2 Outstanding traveler's checks of nonbank issuers
3 Demand deposit balances
4 Negotiable Order of Withdrawal (NOW and Super-NOW) accounts and other checkable deposits.

M2 is the sum of the following:

1 M1
2 Time and savings deposits in amounts under $100,000
3 Individual holdings in money market mutual funds
4 Money market deposit accounts (MMDAs).

M3 was the sum of the following:

1 M2
2 Time deposits at commercial banks in amounts of $100,000 or more
3 Term repurchase agreements
4 Institution-only money market mutual funds
5 Term Eurodollars held by U.S. residents in Canada and the U.K.
6 Overnight retail purchase agreements (Repos)
7 Overnight Eurodollars held by U.S. residents.

Nonfinancial debt is the sum of the following sectors' outstanding debt:

1 U.S. government
2 State and local governments
3 Nonfinancial domestic businesses
4 Households.

References

[1] For institutional information on the Fed, see CRS Report RS20826, *Structure and Functions of the Federal Reserve System*, by Pauline Smale.

[2] It is important to note that this explanation requires the *full employment or structural* budget deficit to rise. Budget deficits produced by a fall in income, or *cyclical* deficits need not produce these results.

[3] Some analysts have argued that the Fed should target a broader measure of financial conditions than the money supply, such as stock prices. See CRS Report RL33666, *Asset Bubbles: Economic Effects Policy Options for the Federal Reserve*, by Marc Labonte.

[4] For a discussion of these studies and the issues involved, see CRS Report RL3 1416, *Monetary Aggregates: Their Use in the Conduct of Monetary Policy*, by Marc Labonte and Gail E. Makinen.

[5] The real rate of interest is determined by the interaction of saving and investment. Thus, change in the national saving rate or the desire to invest can affect the real rate independent of anything the Federal Reserve does. Such changes to the real rate can further complicate the use of interest rates as an indicator of the posture of monetary policy.

[6] For a detailed discussion, see CRS Report RL30904, *Why is the Amount of Currency in Circulation Rising?*, by Marc Labonte and Gail Makinen.

[7] *Monetary Policy Report to the Congress*, February 15, 2006, p. 22.

[8] For more information, see CRS Report RL3 1056, *Economics of Federal Reserve Independence*, by Marc Labonte.

[9] For a review of the research and criticisms, see CRS Report RL3 1955, *Central Bank Independence and Economic Performance: What Does the Evidence Show?*, by Marc Labonte and Gail Makinen.

[10] See CRS Report 98-16, *Should the Federal Reserve Adopt an Inflation Target?*, by Marc Labonte and Gail Makinen.

[11] See CRS Report RL3 1702, *Price Stability (Inflation Targeting) as the Sole Goal of Monetary Policy: The International Experience*, by Marc Labonte and Gail Makinen.

[12] These projections represent the "central tendency" for each variable, which means that in computing the averages in the table the three highest and lowest projections for each variable are excluded.

In: Monetary Policy at the Cutting Edge
Editor: Sarah R. Porter, pp. 21-63
ISBN: 978-1-60692-321-4

Chapter 2

FEDERAL RESERVE BANK OF NEW YORK STAFF REPORTS: OPTIMAL MONETARY POLICY UNDER SUDDEN STOPS*

*Vasco Cúrdia**

ABSTRACT

Emerging market economies often face sudden stops in capital inflows or reduced access to the international capital market. This paper analyzes what monetary policy should accomplish in such an event. Optimal monetary policy induces higher interest rates and exchange rate depreciation. The interest rate hike discourages borrowing and consumption, mitigating the impact of the increased cost of borrowing. The exchange rate depreciation provides a boost to export revenues, reducing the need for, but not averting, a domestic recession. The paper shows that the arrival of the sudden stop further aggravates the time inconsistency problem. Optimal policy is fairly well approximated by a flexible targeting rule, which stabilizes a basket composed of domestic price inflation, exchange rate and

---

* This is an edited, excerpted and augmented edition of a *Federal Reserve Bank of New York Staff Reports*, no. 323 April 2008 publication.

* Vasco Cúrdia: Federal Reserve Bank of New York (e-mail: vasco.curdia@ny.frb.org). The author thanks Michael Woodford for guidance and fruitful discussions. He also gratefully acknowledges suggestions and comments from Roc Armenter, Andrea Ferrero, Chris Sims, and Lars Svensson. The views expressed in this paper are those of the author and do not necessarily reflect the position of the Federal Reserve Bank of New York or the Federal Reserve System.

output. We show that from a welfare perspective, the success of a fixed exchange rate regime depends on the economic environment. For the benchmark parameterization, the peg performs the worst of the simple rules considered. For alternative parameterizations that feature low nominal rigidities or high elasticity of foreign demand, the fixed exchange rate regime performs relatively better.

Keywords: sudden stops, monetary policy, emerging markets, financial crises.

1. Introduction

Emerging market economies are typically characterized as unstable environments subject to a variety of shocks that either do not affect the more developed countries or that are magnified due to lack of credibility of these economies. Caballero (2001) documents some of these issues and reaches the important conclusion that many of the problems of these economies are related to the recurrent loss of access to the international capital markets. Some of the episodes can go as far as to lead to an outbreak of sudden and sharp reversals in the financial account, the sort of which are described as "sudden stops" of capital inflows in the literature, following Calvo (1998).

These shocks affect the production capacity of the economy by restricting the sources for financing investment and imported inputs and thus increasing costs. The subsequent adjustment requires a reversal of the current account usually accompanied by a contraction in economic activity as a corollary of the increased cost of borrowing.[1] The reduction in capital inflows also puts significant pressure on the exchange rate leading to significant devaluations and increased interest rates in order to reduce the draining of capital. As mentioned in Fraga et al. (2003) the shocks augment the trade-offs behind the conduct of monetary policy leading to higher volatility of inflation, output and interest rates.

The literature discusses extensively what the best policy regime for emerging markets might be (e.g. Mishkin (2000) and Mishkin and Savastano (2002)). This paper contributes to this literature by conducting a normative analysis of monetary policy in response to a sudden stop shock. In particular it looks at what is the optimal policy but it also discusses how do several simple rules rank amongst themselves and in comparison to the optimal policy. Furthermore, it discusses

[1] Calvo and Reinhart (2000) documment very well the dimension of these shocks and their consequences to the economy.

what the optimal simple rules are under alternative parameterizations and what is their performance relative to the optimal policy (not constrained to be a simple rule).

Optimal policy should be understood as a benchmark for policy analysis and should entail a reaction to economic conditions that is not dependent on the timing of commitment. Otherwise authorities would always make a new "commitment" every period, losing credibility and eventually getting to be in discretion scenario, rather than in a true commitment. Therefore this paper considers optimal monetary policy in a "timeless perspective" as proposed in Woodford (1999). This criterion has the advantage that we constrain the set of alternatives to time-consistent policies, which adds credibility to them. The analysis thus avoids the time inconsistency problem typical in forward-looking models.[1]

Following the framework proposed in Ciirdia (2007), the economy is subject to shocks in foreigners' perceptions about the performance of the economy. These shocks lead to increases in the required risk premium demanded from domestic borrowers. This is modeled using a modified version of the financial accelerator initially proposed by Bernanke et al. (1999) and applied to an open economy by Gertler et al. (2003). The sudden stop is therefore considered to be exogenous to the economy and is unexpected, similarly to most of the literature on the subject.

In the event of a misperception shock the contraction in the financial account must be matched with an increase in the current account. This can be achieved in two ways: an increase in export revenues and/or a reduction in import expenditures. Optimal policy uses both. A common feature, across most parameterizations of the model, is that optimal monetary policy implies a depreciation of the domestic currency together with increased interest rates. The timing of the two can vary depending on the parameter configuration. In all parameterizations optimal policy implies a real depreciation of the currency. In most of the scenarios considered this is implemented through a nominal depreciation. In the baseline scenario the interest rates are kept low initially, when the shock arrives, but increase significantly one period later.

The optimal policy just described implies that the interest rate increase imposes some adjustment on the part of the domestic economy towards less borrowing and consumption (of both domestic and foreign goods) and the real depreciation leads to increased export revenues and fewer imports. Therefore the current account is adjusting through both imports and exports. This contrasts to the case of a fixed exchange rate system in which the real exchange rate is not

[1] The time inconsistency of optimal policy dates back to the work of Kydland and Prescott (1977).

allowed to adjust as quickly forcing more of the adjustment on the domestic economy and imposing a stronger recession, that in this setting is also welfare reducing.

Optimal policy does not close the output gap as suggested in Hevia (2006) precisely because of the two distortions affecting the economy: monopolistic competition and the imperfect capital market. In order to oppose the two interferences Hevia (2006) finds that a labor tax should be used to eliminate the distortions from monopolistic competition and a capital tax to reduce the distortions from the imperfect capital market. Here none of those are present, leading to a negative output gap on impact, followed by a positive and persistent output gap.

The optimal path of the interest rate compares to the results of Braggion et al. (2005). These authors consider an economy that in normal circumstances has no credit constraints but is subject to the sudden imposition of collateral constraints limiting the availability of credit. Optimal policy under their calibration implies an increase of the interest rate on impact and subsequent gradual reduction, converging in the long run to levels below those verified before the arrival of the shock. In this paper the interest rate also increases (if not on impact at least one period afterwards) and also has a gradual fall. However it will not settle on levels below the initial steady state. The reason for these different results is that Braggion et al. (2005) assumes a permanent shock while here the shocks is expected to eventually disappear. Interestingly the interest rate does converge to the steady state level from below, implying that after the initial increase the interest rate will stay for time at levels just below the steady state ones.

The advantage of the framework used here is its big flexibility and easiness of use to compare alternative policies. In particular we can analyze the extent to which the sudden stop affects the time inconsistency pressures on policy. In particular we can compare the "timeless perspective" with the policy implied by a new commitment when the sudden stop arrives, sometimes also called Ramsey optimal policy. The timeless perspective optimal is time-consistent, while the Ramsey optimal is not as it ignores the expectations of agents formed in previous periods. A Ramsey policy exploits the export revenues dimension even further and delays the recession by one period, as long as there are enough nominal rigidities in the export sector. It does so by using a much larger devaluation and keeping initial interest rates lower. However, if nominal rigidities in the export sector are not present then the cost of using the devaluation channel increases because it translates into stronger cost pressures in the domestic retail sector and thus the Ramsey policy follows a path more consistent to the optimal path under "timeless perspective."

A comparison of simple rules shows that, from a welfare perspective, a peg is not the most desirable regime in the benchmark parametrization. In this parametrization, the peg is actually the worst of the simple rules considered. However, when considering alternative parameterizations, namely those featuring low nominal rigidities or high elasticity of foreign demand, the fixed exchange rate regime performs much better. Given that these are not unreasonable parameterizations the peg should not be eliminated from the list of possible monetary policy strategies to consider when addressing a sudden stop event. This is an important outcome because it shows that whether a fixed exchange rate regime is a good policy depends on the economic environment (or in the model, on the parametrization).

The class of rules considered include two broad types. The first consists of interest rate rules resembling the Taylor rule proposed in Taylor (1993), augmented to include some reaction to the exchange rate. The second group consists of targeting rules aimed at stabilizing inflation but also output and the exchange rate. A general result is that, within the class of rules considered, none manages to strictly implement the optimal policy. However a targeting rule aimed at stabilizing at the same time domestic price inflation, the exchange rate and output is the optimal simple rule and can get very close to the optimal policy. The weights on stabilizing the three components of the basket vary depending on the parameter configuration. In the baseline calibration the weight on inflation far outweights the other two, with the exchange rate receiving very small weight.

In the baseline calibration (and also for low elasticities of foreign demand) the optimal policy can close up to 98% of the welfare gap between the worst rule and the optimal policy (where worst policy is in this scenario the exchange rate peg). Consistent with this, the best rule implies paths for the variables that very closely resemble those under the optimal policy, especially so for the real variables (nominal variables' paths are not exactly matched). These two results together imply that even though flexible inflation targeting is not strictly the optimal policy it gets fairly close to implement it.

Many authors suggest inflation targeting for emerging markets - some examples are Mishkin and Savastano (2002), Caballero and Krishnamurthy (2005) and Fraga et al. (2003). Several emerging markets have successfully implemented inflation targeting frameworks (e.g. Chile and Brazil). The results presented here can be used to suggest that such regimes might be good policy frameworks for emerging markets also when it comes to coping with sudden stops. Indeed it can be argued that the sudden stop affecting Brazil in 2001 was short lived. Whether it was so due to the inflation targeting regime or not is not entirely clear but it is a fact that Brazil has been in recent years more resilient to political shocks that could escalate into crises as its history suggests.

This is not the only paper that looks at how alternative policy regimes cope with shocks to the credit conditions of an emerging market. The literature is actually fairly rich in such exercises. A short list of the ones more closely related are Gertler et al. (2003), Céspedes et al. (2004), Cook (2004), Devereux et al. (2006) and Ciirdia (2007). Most of these focus on a stabilization perspective. Devereux et al. (2006) is the only one which ranks the alternatives according to welfare. Cook (2004) is the only one in which economic conditions might suggest that a peg is the best regime, while all others show that flexible exchange rates and some rule in which interest rates react to inflation and output perform better. However none of the exercises makes an explicit comparison to the optimal policy. Furthermore none of the above consider targeting rules (except to the extent that a peg is itself very particular targeting rule). Therefore this paper presents a more comprehensive analysis of optimal monetary policy in a consistent framework. It is especially noteworthy the ability of this framework in studying under which environments does the fixed exchange rate regime perform better or worse.

The remainder of the paper is organized as follows. Section 2 presents the model in detail. Section 3 discusses the optimal monetary policy and compares it to the flexible price equilibrium. This is followed by an analysis of how different simple rules perform, in section 4. Section 5 concludes.

2. The Model

The model follows very closely Ciirdia (2007). The main distinction is that here there is pricing to market and local currency pricing.[1] Some functional forms were also simplified for the sake of simplicity. The domestic economy is populated by a representative household, firms and the monetary authority. The households consume, provide labor for the production of the domestic good and are the shareholders of the firms of the economy. The domestic good is produced in a perfectly competitive wholesale market. Retail firms then purchase the domestic good from the wholesale firms, convert it into their own varieties, and operate in a monopolistic competition environment setting prices, which are

[1] This change does not change the broad picture of the economic dynamics but is crucial for the ability to characterize optimal monetary policy. Without PTM-LCP the .rst order and

sticky a la Calvo. Each retail firm will sell its variety of the domestic goods to both the domestic and foreign households. However they will set prices differently in the two markets. Furthermore they will set prices in the local currency where the goods is being sold. The foreigners fulfill four roles: they sell inputs and lend money to the wholesale firms, they sell a final good to the domestic households and they purchase the domestic good. The remainder of this section describes in detail the model.[1]

2.1. Households

The representative household derives utility from consumption and disutility from labor, according to

$$\sum_{t=0}^{\infty} \beta^t U(C_t, L_t) \tag{2.1.}$$

where C t refers to consumption and Lt to labor, and

$$U(C_t, L_t) = \frac{C_t^{1-\sigma}}{1-\sigma} - \frac{L_t^{1+\psi}}{1+\psi}.$$

The budget is spent in consumption (with P_t denoting the consumption price index, CPI) and investment in domestic assets, D_t, which pay a return rate of R_t. The domestic assets exist in zero net supply so that, in equilibrium, $D_t = 0$ at all times. The sources of income are the wage collected, W_t, profits from wholesalers, $\pi_{w,t}$, pro.ts from the retailers, $\pi_{w,t}$,[2] and returns on domestic asset holdings:

second order conditions are not satis.ed. Furthermore some parameters also were changed for the same reason.

[1] For easier reading of the paper I insert in appendix A tables listing all the variables (Table 1) and parameters (Table 2) of the model.

[2] Profits are de.ned more formally as $\pi_{w,t} \equiv \int_0^1 \pi_{w,t}(j)\, dj$ and $\pi_{r,t} \equiv \int_0^1 \pi_{r,t}(j)\, dj$.

$$P_t C_t + D_t \leq R_{t-1} D_{t-1} + W_t L_t + \pi_{w,t} + \pi_{r,t}. \tag{2.2}$$

There is a no-Ponzi games condition, so that the problem is well defined,

$$\lim_{T\to\infty} \prod_{s=0}^{T-1} R_{t+s}^{-1} D_{t+T} \geq 0.$$

The households are restricted from accessing the international capital markets and, therefore, cannot borrow or lend to foreigners. The only way households achieve some consumption smoothing is through their holdings of .rms. These can use their net worth to borrow in the international capital market and give higher or lower dividends to their shareholders, the households. In spite of no direct access to foreign credit, there is still some indirect access, through firms' leverage.

The representative household maximizes (2.1) subject to (2.2). The resulting Euler equation for consumption is

$$\frac{1}{R_t} = \beta E_t \left[\frac{C_{t+1}^{-\sigma}}{C_t^{-\sigma}} \frac{1}{\Pi_{t+1}} \right], \tag{2.3}$$

with

$$\Pi_t = P_t / P_{t-1}$$

denoting gross in.ation. Labor supply is described as

$$\frac{W_t}{P_t} = L_t^{\psi} C_t^{\sigma}, \tag{2.4}$$

with W_t the nominal wage.

The households consumption bundle is composed by domestic and foreign goods denoted by $C_{h,t}$ and $C_{f,t}$, respectively. Preferences over the two goods are Cobb-Douglas:

$$C_t = \left(\frac{C_{H,t}}{\gamma}\right)^{\gamma} \left(\frac{C_{F,t}}{1-\gamma}\right)^{1-\gamma} \tag{2.5}$$

The domestic good is purchased at price $P_{h,t}$. The law of one price is assumed for the imported .nal good, here assumed to be the same as the foreign CPI,P_t^* , which for simplicity is set to one at all times. Foreign currency denominated values are converted to domestic currency at the rate S_t. Cost minimization implies the following consumption schedules

$$C_{H,t} = \gamma \frac{P_t C_t}{P_{H,t}}, \tag{2.6}$$

$$C_{F,t} = (1-\gamma) \frac{P_t C_t}{S_t}, \tag{2.7}$$

and the CPI is given by

$$P_t = P_{H,t}^{\gamma} S_t^{1-\gamma}. \tag{2.8}$$

2.2. Wholesale Firms

Wholesale firms operate as price takers in a competitive market. They hire labor, L_t, and purchase an imported input, Z_t, that is required for production but takes one period to process and be used.[1] The technology used by .rm j is given by:

---

1 The convention is that time subscript t denotes variables known at t. Hence, Z_t is the amount of imported input that is bought in period t, but available for use in period t + 1.

$$Y_t(j) = \left(\frac{L_t(j)}{\alpha}\right)^{\alpha} \left(\frac{\omega_t(j) Z_{t-1}(j)}{1-\alpha}\right)^{1-\alpha} \quad (2.9)$$

where $\omega_t(j)$ is an idiosyncratic shock to the productivity of the imported input that is i.i.d. across .rms and time, with $E[\omega_t(j)] = 1$, and is assumed to have a log-normal distribution,

$$(\omega_{t+1}(j)) \sim N\left(-\tfrac{1}{2}\sigma_{\omega}^2, \sigma_{\omega}^2\right)$$

Given the available imported inputs, the labor demand can be expressed as

$$L_t(j) = \alpha \frac{P_{w,t} Y_t(j)}{W_t}, \quad (2.10)$$

where $P_{w;t}$ is the wholesale price of the domestic good.

Define $R_{Z;t+1}(j)$ as the gross returns from investing one domestic currency unit in the imported input:

$$R_{Z,t+1}(j) \equiv (1-\alpha) \frac{P_{w,t+1} Y_{t+1}(j)}{S_t Z_t(j)} \quad (2.11)$$

with the imported inputs purchased at the foreign price level of one.[1] Given the current assumptions for the production function, it is possible to show that we can write

$$R_{Z,t+1}(j) = \omega_{t+1}(j) R_{Z,t+1}, \quad (2.12)$$

[1] Once more assuming the price of imported inputs to be the same as foreign CPI, and this to be one at all times is just for simplicity, without any loss of generality for the analysis in this paper.

where $R_{Z;t+1}$ is the aggregate component, common to all firms.

At the end of the period each .rm has available net worth in domestic currency, N_t (j).

In order to .nance the imports of inputs for the next period it borrows from foreigners the di¤erence between the value of its net worth and the expenditures in the imports. The debt to foreigners, B_t, is denominated in foreign currency, typical of emerging market economies (denominated the "original sin"). The balance sheet of the .rm is given by

$$S_t B_t (j) = S_t Z_t (j) - N_t (j) \tag{2.13}$$

Foreign lenders have misperceptions about the distribution of the imported input productivity ω_{t+1} (j). This Knightian uncertainty is represented as

$$\omega^*_{t+1} (j) = \omega_{t+1} (j) \kappa_t, \tag{2.14}$$

where ω^*_{t+1} (j) refers to foreigners perceptions about ω_{t+1} (j) and _t is the misperception factor. If $k_t = 1$ then there is no misperception (the normal case); and if $k_t \neq 1$ then the perceived distribution is di¤erent from the true one. During sudden stop periods, ambiguity about the distribution for the next period can be described by allowing k_t to have support over a given interval of values, $[k_{ss}, k^{ss}]$. Lenders deal with the Knightian uncertainty through a max-min criterion, as in Gilboa and Schmeidler (1989), or, in other words, that in the face of uncertainty about the underlying distribution they will pick the worst case scenario. This is what can be interpreted as "ambiguity aversion" as described in Backus et al. (2004). As a consequence, in a sudden stop period, they will take the worst case scenario, k_{ss}, as the mean of the distribution of ω_{t+1} (j), instead of one.

The sudden stop is then de.ned as the state in which foreign lenders face the Knightian uncertainty, a state denoted by $S_t = U$. The normal state, is denoted by $S_t = N$. Before any shock takes place the economy is in state St = N. A change to $S_t = U$ is unexpected by the agents. If a sudden stop takes place, there is a probability of reverting to the normal state, given by $\Pr [S_{t+1} = N | S_t = U] = \delta n$.

Once the economy returns to its normal state, a shift back to $S_t = U$ cannot occur and therefore this is a one time sudden stop.[1]

The risk free opportunity cost for the foreigners is the international interest rate, R*, assumed to be constant. However that is not the interest rate charged to the firms on their debt, because of the uncertain productivity of the .rms, implying risk for the creditors. The foreign lenders are risk neutral (after the knightian uncertainty is sorted out). Following Bernanke and Gertler (1989), the problem is set as one of "costly state veri.cation." This implies that, in order to verify the realized idiosyncratic return, the lender has to pay a cost, consisting of a fraction of those returns, so that the total cost of veri.cation, in foreign currency, is

$$\mu \frac{\omega_{t+1}(j) R_{Z,t+1} S_t Z_t(j)}{S_{t+1}}.$$

The debt contract is, then, characterized by a default threshold and a contractual interest rate. A standard debt contract is assumed, implying that the interest rate is not state contingent but the default threshold is (only when firms cannot fulfill their obligations will they default).

The default threshold, $\bar{\omega}_{t+1}(j)$, is set to the level of returns that is just enough to fulfill the debt contract obligations,

$$\frac{\bar{\omega}_{t+1}(j) R_{Z,t+1} S_t Z_t(j)}{S_{t+1}} = R_{B,t}(j) B_t(j), \tag{2.4}$$

where $R_{b,t}$ (j) is the contractual rate of the loan, set in the contract written in period t, and $R_{z,t+1} S_t Z_t$ (j) the operational pro.ts in units of domestic currency. If the idiosyncratic shock is greater than or equal to $\bar{\omega}_{t+1}(j)$, then the .rm repays the loan and collects the remainder of the profits, equal to

$$\omega_{t+1}(j) R_{Z,t+1} S_t Z_t(j) - S_{t+1} R_{B,t}(j) B_t(j).$$

[1] This structure is assumed purposefully to simplify the analysis, leaving extensions of the arrival and exit of the sudden stop for later research.

Otherwise, it declares default, foreign lenders pay the auditing cost and collect everything there is to collect, and the .rm receives nothing. Because foreign lenders are risk neutral, their participation constraint takes the form of

$$\begin{aligned} R^* B_t(j) &= E_t\left[(1 - F^*(\bar{\omega}_{t+1}(j))) R_{B,t}(j) B_t(j)\right] \\ &+ (1-\mu) E_t\left[\int_0^{\bar{\omega}_{t+1}(j)} \omega^* \frac{R_{Z,t+1} S_t Z_t(j)}{S_{t+1}} dF^*(\omega^*)\right], \end{aligned}$$

where F*(.) denotes the distribution of ω_{t+1} (j), as perceived by foreigners. Following Cúrdia (2007), the previous expression can be rewritten as

$$E_t\left[\Omega(\bar{\omega}_{t+1}(j);\kappa_t) R_{Z,t+1} \frac{S_t}{S_{t+1}} Z_t(j)\right] = R^* B_t(j), \tag{2.16}$$

with

$$\Omega(\bar{\omega};\kappa) = \kappa\left[\Gamma\left(\frac{\bar{\omega}}{\kappa}\right) - \mu G\left(\frac{\bar{\omega}}{\kappa}\right)\right], \tag{2.17}$$

$$\Gamma(\bar{\omega}) = [1 - F(\bar{\omega})]\bar{\omega} + \int_0^{\bar{\omega}} \omega dF(\omega), \tag{2.18}$$

$$G(\bar{\omega}) = \int_0^{\bar{\omega}} \omega dF(\omega), \tag{2.19}$$

and F (.) denotes the actual distribution of

$$\omega_{t+1}, \Gamma(\bar{\omega}_t)$$

the fraction of the operation profits used to repay the debt and

$$\mu G(\bar{\omega}_t)$$

the fraction used to pay for the monitoring costs. Therefore

$$\Omega\left(\bar{\omega}_{t+1};\kappa_t\right)$$

is the fraction of the operational pro.ts that foreign lenders perceive that they will keep for themselves after paying the auditing costs.

Firms' cash flows, distributed as dividends to the households, are defined as

$$\Pi_{w,t}(j) \equiv P_{w,t}Y\left(L_t(j), Z_{t-1}(j)\right) - W_tL_t(j) - S_tR_{B,t}(j)\,B_{t-1}(j) - N_t(j),$$

or, equivalently,[1]

$$\Pi_{w,t}(j) = \omega_t(j)\,R_{Z,t}S_{t-1}Z_{t-1}(j) - S_tR_{B,t}(j)\left(Z_{t-1}(j) - \frac{N_{t-1}(j)}{S_{t-1}}\right) - N_t(j).$$

Given the state contingent nature of the optimal contract, the expected cash flow of the firm is

$$E_{t-1}\Pi_{w,t}(j) = E_{t-1}\left\{\left[1 - \Gamma\left(\bar{\omega}_t(j)\right)\right]R_{Z,t}S_{t-1}Z_{t-1}(j) - N_t(j)\right\}. \quad (2.20)$$

Firms maximize the discounted sum of cash .ows,

$$E_0\sum_{t=1}^{\infty}\beta^t\Lambda_t\pi_{w,t}(j),$$

subject to the participation constraint, (2.16), and the default threshold definition, (2.15), with respect to $Z_t(j)$, $\omega_t(j)$, $R_{b;t\_1}(j)$ and N_t (j). The appropriate discount factor is given by $\beta^t\Lambda_t$, from the households problem, where

$$\Lambda_t = C_t^{-\sigma}/P_t$$

---

[1] Using the balance sheet equation and the assumption of constant returns to scale.

is the Lagrangian multiplier of the budget constraint.

As detailed in Cúrdia (2007), all .rms will take the same decisions in face of the expectations about the future. Therefore from this point onwards we can refer to the variables in aggregate terms. The aggregate level of dividends is given by

$$\Pi_{w,t} = [1 - \Gamma(\bar{\omega}_t)] R_{Z,t} S_{t-1} Z_{t-1} - N_t, \tag{2.21}$$

which is readily understood as the fraction of the operational pro.ts that is not paid to the foreign lenders and subtracted from the net worth that is needed for financing the imported input.

The aggregate uncovered interest parity (UIP) relationship is given by

$$R_t E_t \left[\frac{C_{t+1}^{-\sigma}}{P_{t+1}} \right] = R^* E_t \left[\frac{C_{t+1}^{-\sigma}}{P_{t+1}} \frac{S_{t+1}}{S_t} \lambda_{t+1} \right], \tag{2.22}$$

which includes the risk premium term, λ_{t+1}, due to the fact that households have access to the international capital market only through leveraged .rms, which might default on their debt. The risk premium term is given, in equilibrium, by

$$\lambda_t = \frac{\Gamma'(\bar{\omega}_t)}{E_{t-1} [\Omega'(\bar{\omega}_t; \kappa_{t-1})]}. \tag{2.23}$$

The aggregate operational pro.t of .rms will, in equilibrium, be enough to pay a premium on the foreign risk free interest rate,

$$E_t \left[\frac{C_{t+1}^{-\sigma}}{P_{t+1}} [1 - \Gamma(\bar{\omega}_{t+1})] R_{Z,t+1} \right] = (1 - b_t) R^* E_t \left[\frac{C_{t+1}^{-\sigma}}{P_{t+1}} \frac{S_{t+1}}{S_t} \lambda_{t+1} \right], \tag{2.24}$$

where b_t is the leverage rate of firms, defined as $b_t / B_t \equiv Z_t$.

2.3. Retail Firms

There is a continuum of size one of retail .rms operating in a monopolistic competition environment. They purchase the domestic good from the representative wholesale firm, at price $P_{w,t}$, convert it at no additional cost into their own variety of the final good and sell it to both the domestic and foreign markets. There is price stickiness a la Calvo so with probability α_p each individual firm is not able to set prices in a given period. There is pricing to market with local currency pricing, so that $P_{H;t}$ denotes prices for the domestic market and $P^*_{H;t}$ the price in the foreign market. We assume identical elasticities for different varieties in both markets.

The preferences of the consumers for the di¤erent varieties of the domestic good are given by

$$Y_t^i = \left(\int_0^1 Y_t^i(j)^{\frac{\eta-1}{\eta}} dj \right)^{\frac{\eta}{\eta-1}}$$

with $\eta > 1$ in order to imply elasticity of substitution above one. The demand for each variety is given by

$$Y_t^i(j) = Y_t^i \left(\frac{P_{H,t}^i(j)}{P_{H,t}^i} \right)^{-\eta} \tag{2.25}$$

where, in equilibrium, the market must clear and

$$Y_t = C_{H,t} + C_{H,t}^*. \tag{2.26}$$

The global foreign demand for domestic goods has the following form:

$$C_{H,t}^* = \gamma^* \left(P_{H,t}^*\right)^{-\nu^*} C^* \tag{2.27}$$

where C* is the foreign aggregate consumption level. The problem of .rm j in the domestic market is

$$\max_{\bar{P}_{H,t}(j)} E_t \sum_{\tau=0}^{\infty} \alpha_p^{\tau} \beta^{\tau} \Lambda_{t+\tau} C_{H,t+\tau} \left(\frac{\bar{P}_{H,t}(j)}{P_{H,t+\tau}} \right)^{-\eta} \left(\bar{P}_{H,t}(j) - P_{w,t+\tau} \right),$$

with

$$\bar{P}_{H,t}(j)$$

denoting the price set in period t. The .rst order condition is

$$\bar{P}_{H,t} = \frac{\eta}{\eta - 1} \frac{E_t \sum_{\tau=0}^{\infty} \alpha_p^{\tau} \beta^{\tau} \frac{C_{t+\tau}^{-\sigma}}{P_{t+\tau}} C_{H,t+\tau} P_{H,t+\tau}^{\eta} P_{w,t+\tau}}{E_t \sum_{\tau=0}^{\infty} \alpha_p^{\tau} \beta^{\tau} \frac{C_{t+\tau}^{-\sigma}}{P_{t+\tau}} C_{H,t+\tau} P_{H,t+\tau}^{\eta}}, \tag{2.28}$$

where I used the fact that all .rms able to set a new price at time t will choose exactly the same one. The aggregate domestic price index (DPI) is

$$P_{H,t} = \left[(1 - \alpha_p) \bar{P}_{H,t}^{1-\eta} + \alpha_p P_{H,t-1}^{1-\eta} \right]^{\frac{1}{1-\eta}}. \tag{2.29}$$

For the price setting in the export market we get equivalently

$$\max_{\bar{P}_{H,t}^{*}(j)} E_t \sum_{\tau=0}^{\infty} \alpha_p^{\tau} \beta^{\tau} \Lambda_{t+\tau} C_{H,t+\tau}^{*} \left(\frac{\bar{P}_{H,t}^{*}(j)}{P_{H,t+\tau}^{*}} \right)^{-\eta} \left(S_{t+\tau} \bar{P}_{H,t}^{*}(j) - P_{w,t+\tau} \right),$$

and note that because price is set in foreign currency, $S_t P^*_{H;t}$ (j), is the domestic currency value of each unit of exports. The .rst order condition is given by

$$\bar{P}^*_{H,t} = \frac{\eta}{\eta-1} \frac{E_t \sum_{\tau=0}^{\infty} \alpha_p^{\tau} \beta^{\tau} \frac{C_{t+\tau}^{-\sigma}}{P_{t+\tau}} C^*_{H,t+\tau} \left(P^*_{H,t+\tau}\right)^{\eta} P_{w,t+\tau}}{E_t \sum_{\tau=0}^{\infty} \alpha_p^{\tau} \beta^{\tau} \frac{C_{t+\tau}^{-\sigma}}{P_{t+\tau}} C^*_{H,t+\tau} \left(P^*_{H,t+\tau}\right)^{\eta} S_{t+\tau}},$$

and the aggregate price index is

$$P^*_{H,t} = \left[(1-\alpha_p)\left(\bar{P}^*_{H,t}\right)^{1-\eta} + \alpha_p \left(P^*_{H,t-1}\right)^{1-\eta}\right]^{\frac{1}{1-\eta}}. \quad (2.30)$$

2.4. Monetary Policy

The role of the monetary authority is to control the interest rate, which is a very reasonable assumption given how modern monetary policy is conducted, including in emerging markets, as suggested in Hawkins (2005). In the absence of explicit monetary aggregates, it is possible to think of this economy as in the cashless-limiting case of Woodford (2003).

There are three types of monetary policy that are considered in the analysis: optimal monetary analysis in a timeless perspective, optimal monetary analysis under a new commitment and simple policy rules. The best policy should avoid the time inconsistency problems discussed in Kydland and Prescott (1977) among many others. This is the optimal policy with commitment in a timeless perspective, as proposed in Woodford (1999). It is nevertheless worth considering as well the optimal policy under a new commitment, which is not time consistent, in order to highlight the extent to which the sudden stop affects the time inconsistency of policy. In both cases the monetary authority maximizes the welfare of the households subject to the laws of motion of the economy as described in appendix B.

Finally, several simple rules are considered, including interest rate rules,

$$\frac{R_t}{R} = \left(\Pi_t\right)^{\phi_\pi} \left(\Pi_{H,t}\right)^{\phi_{\pi H}} \left(\frac{S_t}{S_{t-1}}\right)^{\phi_s} \left(\frac{Y_t}{Y}\right)^{\phi_y/4} \quad (2.31)$$

and simple "speci.c targeting rules," in the terminology of Svensson and Woodford (2005).

These involve the stabilization of a basket of variables, each with a given weight and can be represented as

$$1 = (\Pi_t)^{\phi_\pi} (\Pi_{H,t})^{\phi_{\pi H}} \left(\frac{S_t}{S_{t-1}}\right)^{\phi_s} \left(\frac{Y_t}{Y}\right)^{\phi_y/4} \tag{2.32}$$

in which, for the sake parsimony, one of the coe¢ cients is normalized to one.

2.5. General Equilibrium and Parameter Values

The resources of this economy are determined by the budget constraint of the representative household. If we substitute out the pro.ts from .rms and making a few other manipulations we convert the budget constraint into the balance of payments (BP) of this economy:

$$0 = S_t P^*_{H,t} C^*_{H,t} - S_t C_{F,t} - S_t Z_t - \Gamma(\bar{\omega}_t) R_{Z,t} S_{t-1} Z_{t-1} + S_t B_t. \tag{2.33}$$

Finally it.s important to note that only relative prices are determined and therefore inflation rates and real variables shall be analyzed henceforth. In particular, more important than the nominal interest rate is the real interest rate,

$$R^r_t = E_t \left[R_t / \Pi_{t+1}\right]$$

the real return on imported inputs,

$$R^r_{Z,t} = R_{Z,t} / \Pi_t$$

and the DPI inflation,

$$\Pi_{H,t} = P_{H,t} / P_{H,t-1}.$$

The relative prices are all normalized by the domestic CPI and represented by small caps: the real exchange rate, s_t, the real wage rate, w_t, the relative wholesale prices, $p_{w;t}$, the relative price of the domestic good, $p_{H;t}$, and real net worth, n_t.[1] The list of all equations using real variables is shown in appendix B.

The structural parameter values used follow closely those of Cúrdia (2007), except that some of them were set to values more stylized for easiness of analysis. All of the parameters are listed in appendix 3 and are used in all experiments except when otherwise noted. One parameter in particular is of importance here, the foreign demand price elasticity, which is set to one in the baseline scenario. This parameter is considered to be very important, in particular to the outcomes of the economy in terms of output. Therefore even though the baseline case takes this elasticity to be unity, a special parameter sensitivity of the results is discussed below.

The solution method depends on the analysis being conducted. For the simple rules the model is log-linearized around the zero in.ation steady state, which coincides with the optimal steady state. After log-linearization all variables are denoted by

$$\hat{x}_t = \ln(x_t/x)$$

with x denoting the steady state value of the variable. For the optimal policy under a new commitment the solution is computed in two steps: derivation of the FOC based on the nonlinear equations, followed by log-linearization of all the equations in order to generate the solution to the rational expectations equilibrium (REE). The policy in a timeless perspective uses the linear quadratic approximation method proposed in Benigno and Woodford (2006).

3. Optimal Monetary Policy

The response of the economy to a sudden stop are thoroughly described in Cúrdia (2007) as well as the comparison of the impact of di¤erent policies in those responses. Here the object of interest is to characterize the optimal monetary policy under full commitment. Optimal behavior of the monetary authority should be considered in a framework in which the commitment is credible to the economic agents. A good way to earn the desired credibility is precisely by choosing a policy behavior that is consistent over time, conditional on the occurrence of shocks. Therefore optimal policy is characterized by the choice of

[1] The price of exports would be normalized by the foreign CPI but it is assumed that P^*_t is

paths for the variables such that they maximize the welfare of the households subject to the laws of motion of the economy and a pre-commitment constraints that enforce time consistency of policy. This is the timeless perspective described in Woodford (1999) and formalized in Benigno and Woodford (2007).

Besides a time-consistent optimal policy it is also useful to consider optimal policy under a commitment that is not time-consistent. This helps understanding the extent to which the sudden stop a¤ects the commitment problem. Such alternative policy is labeled here as Ramsey. Therefore this section compares optimal policy with and without time consistency, keeping the .exible price equilibrium in the background, as a benchmark. The impulse response functions (IRF's) in these three cases are presented in figures 1 and 2. These show the responses of the economy to a misperceptions shock, in log-deviations[1] relative to the scenario without shocks.[2] Further notice that nominal variables in the .ex-price equilibrium depend on the policy conducted and hence are not shown for lack of relevance.

According to these .gures the optimal policy implies that the interest rate is initially kept relatively stable, while there is a devaluation of the domestic currency. One period after the interest rate is sharply increased and afterwards is gradually stabilized back to pre-shock levels. This policy leads to a strong contraction of consumption and output, with the latter falling by a smaller amount due to an increase in exports. In.ation initially increases but afterwards is roughly stabilized.

The first lesson from this exercise is immediate result that optimal policy is far from enforcing a .xed exchange rate regime. This is relevant because in several episodes of sudden stops the authorities tried to enforce precisely such a regime, failing in most cases and then allowing finally the currency to devalue. Instead, according to the results presented here they should immediately devalue, followed by the stabilization of the currency by increasing the interest rate, not the other way around.

The reasoning behind the optimal policy is as follows. The sudden stop is in fact a negative supply shock in that it increases the cost of acquiring inputs

constant at all times and therefore that would be a meaningless normalization.

1 All paths are multiplied by one hundred to give an interpretation of percentage deviations. The in.ation and interest rates are further multiplied by four in order to yield annualized rate changes.

2 For .exible prices and the optimal policy the evolution under no sudden stop shock is just the steady state itself. However, under Ramsey there is a deviation from steady state in the initial period even in the absence of any shocks. This is due to the time inconsistency of the policy, which is not consistent with the steady state.

necessary to produce, by increasing the cost of .nancing it. This implies that there is a contraction in the financial account that needs to be matched by an increase in the current account. There are two options to achieve that: to increase export revenues and/or to reduce the value of imports. The option of enforcing a peg implies a substantial increase in the domestic interest rate (unless there are vast amounts of currency reserves, which is not considered here) but that will imply a strong contraction in domestic demand. A better policy is to use both options and contract the value of imports at the same time that the revenues from exports are increased. This is precisely what the optimal policy accomplishes.

Another interesting lesson is that the comparison to the flex-price equilibrium shows that the output gap is negative on impact but persistently positive afterwards. This is consistent with the idea that optimal policy implements some smoothing of the output, relative to the flex-price equilibrium. This translates also into some smoothing of domestic consumption, especially consumption of domestic goods.

This result regarding the path of the interest rate also compares to the work of Braggion et al. (2005). They present a model in which the optimal response to reduced access to the international capital markets is an initial sharp rise in the interest rate followed by a fall to below pre-crisis levels. The reason why in their results the interest rate falls to levels below pre-crisis levels is explained by the fact that the increased requirements for collateral are permanent and therefore the interest rate needs to move to a permanent lower level to discourage borrowing and make the collateral constraint marginally not binding in the new steady state. Instead, here the misperceptions are expected to eventually revert to normal levels and therefore there is no need to make such permanent changes in the interest rate, so that it converges back to the pre-crisis levels. However it is interesting to note that after the spike the interest rates do indeed reach levels lower than the no shock scenario and converge from below. The remainder di¤erence that requires some interpretation is the initial response of the interest rate. They get an optimal immediate increase while here it is kept low. The answer to this is in the parameter con.guration. Figure 3 shows responses when $\alpha_p = 0{:}5$ (instead of $\alpha_p = 0{:}75$), hence implying smaller nominal rigidities. Figure 4 shows responses when the the foreign elasticity of foreign demand is lower with, $v^* = 0{:}6$ (instead of $v^* = 1$).

If nominal rigidities are lower or if the elasticity of foreign demand is lower then both the nominal and real interest rates will spike on impact and then follow a gradual reduction, much like in the baseline scenario (including eventually attaining levels below pre-crisis levels and converging to those levels from below). Noticeably the lower elasticity of foreign demand is considered by some as more realistic for emerging markets (e.g. Reinhart (1994)). Therefore it can be concluded that the results in this model can be considered consistent with those in Braggion et al. (2005).

Looking more closely at these alternative parameterizations we can further conclude that as nominal rigidities are smaller or the elasticity of foreign demand is lower the emphasis is less on the depreciation and more on the impact increase of the interest rate. Regarding the smaller nominal rigidities that ought to be expected given that as the economy gets closer to .exible prices the prices do more of the adjustment towards the required real exchange rate depreciation that is needed and therefore less adjustment in the nominal exchange rate is needed.

The only reason why there is a devaluation of the currency is that it implies higher value of the export revenues. The cost however is that it also increases the cost of imported inputs, creating pressure on costs. Furthermore, it will have also a direct impact on the desired price of exports (set in local currency). If desired lower prices in exports are introduced then there is an increase in foreign demand for the domestic goods, which will lead to higher labor demand and wage pressure. This compounds to generate higher marginal costs and a higher desired prices also in the domestic retail price of the domestic good which will have the negative impact of driving lower consumption of the domestic goods and overall consumption. This mechanism is actually very important for other results but in particular it explains why higher nominal rigidities lead to stronger depreciation rates of the currency. If nominal rigidities are stronger then the transmission from desired prices to actual prices is smaller and therefore the cost of a devaluation is smaller.

It also explains why the elasticity of foreign demand in.uences the optimal policy. If the elasticity is lower then foreign demand will not react as much to the lower foreign prices and therefore the cost of the devaluation will be lower. However the bene.t of the depreciation falls too because this strategy actually implies a fall in revenue in foreign currency (given that the price of exports falls more than the exports' demand increases), so that a bigger depreciation would be needed to attain the same goal. Figure 4 shows that the this reduction in bene.ts is more prevalent than the reduction in costs, hence the smaller devaluation. The reason is that the reduction in bene.ts is not one to one with that in bene.ts, precisely due to nominal rigidities at the level of export price determination. It can be shown that if nominal rigidities are not present in the export sector then a reduction in foreign demand elasticity promotes a bigger devaluation in response to the sudden stop.

It is also relevant to understand to what extent the sudden stop in.uences the time inconsistency problem. For that we can turn again to .gure 1 and compare the responses between the optimal policy and Ramsey. The di¤erence between is immediately obvious: Ramsey implies a much stronger devaluation on impact and much lower interest rates. Indeed this policy manages to increase the value of exports by so much that there is no need to impose a contraction on domestic consumption of the domestic goods. It actually increases so that the consumption basket is actually roughly stabilized. It is also noticeable that in this case output, on impact actually increases. Given that the di¤erence between Ramsey and optimal policy increases we can conclude that the sudden stop generates an even stronger time inconsistency in policy. The reason for this goes back to the bene.ts and costs of a devaluation. The cost is determined by the extent to which the desired price changes are translated into actual price changes and the time inconsistency emerges from the fact that by not taking into account how past expectations were formed, the Ramsey policy exploits this to the extreme. The time consistent optimal policy instead does not exploit it as much precisely due to the commitment to take into account past expectations about current policy behavior.

If we eliminate the nominal rigidities in the foreign export sector (but keep the ones in the domestic retail sector) we get responses as in .gure 5. It shows that the elimination of this type of rigidities leads to a bigger cost of devaluing, so that Ramsey exploits is much less. Curiously the optimal policy implies a slightly stronger devaluation which might be explained by the fact that it is less constrained by past expectations. The overall results is that the time inconsistency, measured loosely as the di¤erence between these two policies is reduced. It is thus very reasonable to conclude that a key driver of why the sudden stop increases the time inconsistency of policy is due to the existence of nominal rigidities in the export sector.

4. SIMPLE RULES

In the literature monetary policy is frequently represented as following simple rules, the most prominent of which is the Taylor rule presented in Taylor (1993). Such rules stipulate that the monetary authority commits to follow a simple rule. Taylor showed that an empirical rule in which the interest rate responds to in.ation and the output deviations from trend is a very good representation of how the US Federal Reserve conducted policy over a period in which monetary policy is generally considered to have done a good job. This however is an empirical statement. Nothing is said about the optimality of such rules. However they are very attractive especially in cases in which monetary policy is not very credible and therefore the monitoring of the compliance to such a simple policy can be tracked by the economic agents. Therefore the obvious question is how well do simple rules perform, relative to the optimal policy, from a welfare perspective. A second issue is the possibility that a simple rule might actually implement the optimal policy or, at least, get very close to the optimal policy. These are precisely the two issues discussed in this section.

4.1. Benchmark Rules

The .rst question that should be posed whenever a simple rule is proposed is how good such a rule is. That will generally depend on the economic structure taking into consideration all the types of shocks that the economy faces. Here the exercise is not so much the discussion of whether such policies are the best to implement in the type of economies under consideration, but a narrower one: how good are those policies in the event of a sudden stop. Furthermore how do di¤erent types of rules compare relative to each other, from a welfare perspective.

Cook (2004) analyzes a similar question by comparing the volatility of some key variables under alternative policy rules. The conclusion is that a peg is more stabilizing than interest rate rules targeting in.ation. Devereux et al. (2006) compare both the volatility of responses as well as the expected welfare and conclude that it is best to have a policy rule in terms of non-traded goods in.ation or in terms of CPI, depending on the pass-through but in any case either of those fares better than an exchange rate peg. Céspedes et al. (2004) and Gertler et al. (2003) perform similar exercises in terms of a response to the foreign interest rate and also conclude that the peg is the worst policy in terms of stabilization of the economy. This section performs a welfare comparison of rules based on the quadratic approximation suggested in Benigno and Woodford (2006).

The rules considered here are those discussed in Cúrdia (2007), starting with a fixed exchange rate regime, or peg, which all of the above authors consider. Two other obvious rules are strict in.ation stabilization in terms of the CPI and in terms of the DPI. Another type of rules usually considered in the literature (e.g. Gertler et al. (2003)) is a Taylor rule reacting to in.ation and output deviations from steady state. This section considers two such rules, one with CPI in.ation (labeled CPI Taylor) and another with DPI in.ation (labeled DPI Taylor). In both of these the coe¢ cient on in.ation is 2 and the coefficient on output is 0.75. Like in Cook (2004) we also consider rules in which the interest rate further reacts to directly to the exchange rate, besides the implicit reaction through the in.ation measure. The resulting rules are the CPI dirty .oat and the DPI dirty float, to convey precisely the idea that these are .exible exchange rate regimes but in which policy pays explicit attention to the exchange rate. In both the coefficient on nominal exchange rate depreciation is 0.5. The resulting welfare comparison is shown in table 4. The first column indicates welfare relative to the level attained by the optimal policy. A value of zero is not readily interpretable but allows us to rank how well the di¤erent policies.

The numbers suggest that the peg is the worst policy among the ones considered and that a DPI Taylor rule is the best of these ones. The welfare level of the peg is not especially relevant because we will not know if attaining 78.8% of the welfare achieved by the optimal policy is a high number or not. However, being the worst policy it allows us to compare the other rules in terms of how much welfare gap between the optimal policy and the peg they are able to close, which is precisely the measure presented in the second column of the table. This allows us to say the DPI Taylor closes about 90.2% of that welfare gap and hence we can say that it improves considerably relative to the peg. The CPI Taylor is also a good policy relative to the peg but not as much as the DPI Taylor. It is also interesting to notice that in this calibration the two dirty .oat rules lead to lower welfare values than the corresponding Taylor rules without reaction to the exchange rate.

The analysis can be further complemented by a comparison of these two rules (the worst and the best out of these ones) with the optimal policy, presented in figure 6. It becomes clear that the peg is not similar to the optimal responses implying double the contraction in output and almost double the contraction in consumption as the optimal policy. The interest rate and real exchange rate are also somewhat di¤erent, with the peg implying a more signi.cant increase in interest rate and a smaller real depreciation. The DPI Taylor rule instead implies paths for the variables that are very similar to those implied by the optimal policy both in terms of the pattern but also quantitatively.

It is important to understand the extent to which the ranking changes for different parameterizations. Therefore three scenarios are considered, much like those considered in the previous section: lower nominal rigidities (α_p = 0:5 in both domestic retail and export sectors), no nominal rigidities in the export sector and two di¤erent elasticities of foreign demand (v* = 0:6 and v* = 20). Table 5 presents the relative welfare in all of these scenarios for each rule. The .rst result worth mentioning is that the peg is not always the worst policy.

In particular, if the nominal rigidities in both sectors are lower or if the elasticity of foreign demand is very high then the it can become the best of these simple rules.

The performance of the peg should not be a surprise. With nominal rigidities, if a peg is enforced then the economy cannot adjust very much to the shock, except by giving time for prices to adjust as larger and larger fractions of .rms adjust their prices. As nominal rigidities get smaller so does the time it takes the prices to perform this adjustment. However if the exchange rate is free to change then the adjustment will be much faster. Therefore lower nominal rigidities should eliminate a big part of the drawbacks of the peg.[1] Given that these are not unreasonable parameterizations the peg should not be eliminated from the list of possible monetary policy strategies to consider when addressing a sudden stop event.

Furthermore, as the foreign demand elasticity increases a fall in the price of exports gets more power, so that a lower devaluation is necessary to accomplish an increase in foreign demand. In the limit the exchange rate is very close to being stabilized because it is not required to expand exports. It is also interesting to notice that the ranking of the peg is even worse if we consider the more realistic scenario of low elasticity of foreign demand. Another interesting result is that if nominal rigidities in exports are eliminated then the best of these rules is to stabilize the DPI price index.

One .nal comment is that under lower nominal rigidities the peg is the best rule but the CPI dirty .oat is also fairly good, so it is possible that in this scenario a dirty float with different coefficients might do better than a pure peg. In the scenario of lower (and more realistic) elasticity of foreign demand the DPI dirty float is actually the highest ranked policy which suggests that a dirty .oat might do a reasonably good job in the event of a sudden stop.

4.2. Optimal Rules

Comparison of simple rules among themselves and with the optimal policy is an informative exercise, but it can be subject to the criticism of why certain coefficients are used instead of others, and whether these in.uence the results. Therefore we now discuss which are the best simple rules within a certain class of rules.

The .rst class of rules considered is the one in which the interest rate reacts to CPI in.ation, output and the exchange rate:

---

[1] This does not mean that it implements the optimal policy in those alternative scenarios or even that it is the best simple rule (which shall be analyzed later). It simply states that the peg performs relatively better than several alternative simple rules.

$$\frac{R_t}{R} = (\Pi_t)^{\phi_\pi} \left(\frac{S_t}{S_{t-1}}\right)^{\phi_s} \left(\frac{Y_t}{Y}\right)^{\phi_y/4}$$

The first immediate result is that it is optimal to set $\varphi_s = 0$, hence the interest rate should not react to the exchange rate more than what is already implied by the CPI.[1] This however is the optimal coefficient if we restrict it to be non-negative. Without this restriction it is optimal to react to the exchange rate less than the implied by reacting to CPI in.ation (a negative coefficient φ_s).

The search for the best coe¢ cients for in.ation and output shows that if both diverge to infinity at a constant ratio then the welfare keeps increasing. This is not a very reasonable rule to implement and it actually suggests that a better policy is to target a combination of in.ation and output stabilization, implied by

$$1 = (\Pi_t)^{\phi_\pi} \left(\frac{Y_t}{Y}\right)^{\phi_y/4}$$

If we normalize $\varphi_\pi = 1$ then the optimal weight on output is $\varphi_y = 3{:}516$, which implies that a one annual percentage point in.ation has the same weight as a 0.28 percentage point output deviation from steady state levels in the targeting basket. Such policy closes about 85.38% of the welfare gap between the peg and the optimal policy. This is an improvement relative to the benchmark CPI Taylor rule but still lower than the welfare levels of the benchmark DPI interest rate rule.

If we consider rules reacting to CPI in.ation and output, but now in terms of the quarterly changes in the output, instead of deviations from steady state we are able to improve on the previous one. The best such rule is an interest rate rule

$$\frac{R_t}{R} = (\Pi_t)^{5.53} \left(\frac{Y_t}{Y_{t-1}}\right)^{6.94}$$

which implies fairly strong interest rate responses to changes in either the in.ation rate or the output growth rate. Such a rule closes 95.31% of the welfare gap between the peg and the optimal policy, which is an improvement relative to the CPI Taylor consider before.

---

1 To better understand this statement, just recall that $P_t = P_{H,t}^{\gamma} S_t^{1-\gamma}$.

Another relevant case is the one in which we consider DPI in.ation, exchange rate depreciation rate and output deviations from steady state,

$$1 = (\Pi_{H,t}) \left(\frac{S_t}{S_{t-1}}\right)^{\phi_s} \left(\frac{Y_t}{Y}\right)^{\phi_y/4}$$

This is relevant because we allow for the di¤erentiated response to DPI in.ation and exchange rate, without restricting to the weights implied in the consumption basket and the comparison of the benchmark rules suggests that a rule based on DPI instead of CPI performs better. The best interest rate rule again implies coefficients diverging to in.nity at constant rates. The best targeting rule, seen also as the limit of the best interest rate rule is to set φ_s = 0:062 and φ_y = 1:511, which implies that one annual percentage point inflation has the same weight as a 4% quarterly exchange rate depreciation or a 0.66% deviation of the output from steady state. Given the big volatility of exchange rates this is a significant reaction to the exchange rate, but it is not as much as implied by the CPI (which would be (1-γ/γ=0.33). Indeed if this rule was converted to CPI targeting rule it would imply a negative weight for the exchange rate.

This rule closes 98.13% the gap between the peg and the optimal policy. This means that even though it doesn.t exactly implement the optimal policy it gets really close. This is con.rmed by a comparison of the impulse response functions presented in figure 7. The two responses are almost identical for all real variables. The nominal ones are somewhat more di¤erent. It should be noted that all the other rules considered yielded lower levels of welfare than this one for the baseline scenario.

Given the optimal simple rule it is important to understand to what extent it is sensitive to some key parameters of this economy. If we consider lower nominal rigidities (α_p = 0:5) in both the export and domestic retail markets then it is optimal to target a combination of exchange rate depreciation and output deviations from steady state,

$$1 = \left(\frac{S_t}{S_{t-1}}\right) \left(\frac{Y_t}{Y}\right)^{1.84}$$

which confirms the previous result that as nominal rigidities are smaller it is better to stabilize the exchange rate. However it should be a .exible stabilization, with some weight given to output deviations from steady state. This .exible criterion improves somewhat on the peg (which is considered above the best of the benchmark rules), closing 76.9% of the welfare gap between DPI stabilization (the worst rule considered) and the optimal policy. This rule however implies responses to the shock that are di¤erent from those implied by the optimal policy.

If we consider that there are no nominal rigidities in the export sector then the best simple rule within the class considered here is to impose DPI stabilization.

Previously we had mentioned that as the elasticity of foreign demand increases the peg becomes a better policy. similarly if we consider the smaller elasticity of foreign demand that might be somewhat more realistic, then the optimal simple rule considered is a flexible targeting criterion of the type considered for the benchmark scenario but in which the coefficients are di¤erent: $\varphi_s = 0.426$ and $\varphi y = 3.583$. In this scenario of low elasticity the worst rule considered is DPI stabilization and the optimal rule closes the welfare gap between that and the optimal policy is 97.8%, implying that it is a very good policy indeed even if it does not exactly implement the optimal policy. Furthermore we can formulate this rule as one in terms of flexible targeting of CPI, with weights in the exchange rate and output:

$$1 = \Pi_t \left(\frac{S_t}{S_{t-1}}\right)^{0.132} \left(\frac{Y_t}{Y}\right)^{0.671}.$$

It is noteworthy that if the elasticity of foreign demand is lower then the exchange rate depreciation gains more weight in the targeting rule, above that implied by the CPI basket, hence the positive coe¢ cient above.

The conclusion is that for reasonable parameter con.gurations the best simple rule is to follow a .exible in.ation targeting rule, with some weight on output deviations from steady state and a weight on the exchange rate relative to the domestic prices that may or may not be below that implied by the CPI basket. In any case this is very simple rule that does not implement the optimal policy but gets really close to achieve that.

5. Conclusion

This paper considered a versatile framework that is reasonable to describe an emerging market and performed comprehensive analysis of optimal monetary policy in response to a sudden stop in capital in.ows.

Optimal monetary policy exploits the export revenues in order to minimize the impact on the domestic economy but the recession is not totally avoided. A domestic currency depreciation is combined with high interest rates to achieve this result. Unless there are no nominal rigidities in the export sector, the arrival of the sudden stop increases the problem of time inconsistency of policy, further strengthening the importance of credibility and commitment for emerging markets.

In a comparison of the optimal policy with simple rules, we conclude that, for the relevant parameterizations, the optimal policy is fairly well approximated by a flexible targeting rule, in which a combination of domestic prices, exchange rate and output are considered. However, the weights on the di¤erent variables are sensitive to parametrization in a non-negligible way.

An important outcome of the paper is to show that whether a .xed exchange rate regime is a good policy depends on the economic environment (or in the model, on the parametrization). For the benchmark parametrization, the peg performs badly, from a welfare perspective. If we consider lower nominal rigidities or high elasticity of foreign demand, then the peg performs much better.

The analysis presented here is fairly broad but it does not close the subject of optimal policy in an emerging market subject to sudden stops. A relevant limitation of it is the consideration of the shock to be completely exogenous. Actually most papers on the matter are subject to this criticism and it would be important to analyze the case in which the arrival of the sudden stop is not exogenous or in which policy can in.uence the duration of such episodes. Caballero and Krishnamurthy (2005) discuss the consequences for monetary policy of the threat of a sudden stop that can occur in the future and how current and future expected policies interact. This type of exercise should be extended further to incorporate more complete frameworks such as the one considered here.

A. Variables and Parameters

Table 1. Variables present in the model

P_t	consumption price index (CPI)	Π_t	CPI inflation rate
$P_{H,t}$	domestic price index (DPI)	$\Pi_{H,t}$	DPI inflation rate
$P^*_{H,t}$	exports price index$^{(1)}$	$p_{H,t}$	relative dom. goods retail price
$P_{w,t}$	wholesale dom. goods price	$p_{w,t}$	wholesale dom. goods relative price
W_t	nominal wage rate	w_t	real wage rate
R_t	domestic interest rate	R^r_t	real interest rate
R^*	foreign risk free interest rate	λ_t	risk premium term
$R_{Z,t}$	returns on imported inputs	$R^r_{Z,t}$	real returns on imported inputs
S_t	nominal exchange rate	s_t	real exchange rate
C_t	consumption bundle	C^*	foreign aggregate consumption
$C_{H,t}$	consumption of domestic goods	$C^*_{H,t}$	foreign consumption of dom. goods
$C_{F,t}$	consumption of foreign goods	Y_t	domestic goods production
L_t	labor	Z_t	imported inputs
B_t	debt$^{(1)}$	b_t	leverage ratio
$\omega_t(j)$	imported input productivity shock	$\omega^*_t(j)$	foreigners perceptions about $\omega_t(j)$
$\bar{\omega}_t$	default threshold	$R_{B,t}$	gross interest rate in debt contract
$\pi_{r,t}$	profits of retail firms	$\pi_{w,t}$	profits of wholesale firms
N_t	nominal net worth	n_t	real net worth
D_t	domestic assets	κ_t	misperception factor

(1) de.ned in foreign currency.

Table 2. Parameters present in the model

β	discount factor
σ	inverse of the intertemporal elasticity of substitution
ψ	inverse of the labor supply elasticity
γ	share of the domestic good in the consumption under unit elasticity of substitution
α	share of labor to the production of the domestic goods under unit elasticity of substitution
σ^2_ω	variance of the log-normal distribution of ω
μ	monitoring costs
δ_n	probability of exit from sudden stop
κ_{ss}	misperception factor during sudden stop
η	elasticity of substitution among the different varieties of the domestic goods
ν^*	foreign demand price elasticity
γ^*	share of the domestic good in the foreign consumption under unit elasticity of substitution
α_p	probability that a firm is not able to set prices in a given period

Table 3. Parameter values

β	0.98401	α	0.5	ν^*	1	μ	0.019065
σ	1	α_p	0.75	γ^*	0.1	σ_ω	0.392202
ψ	2	η	6	C^*	5	δ_n	0.10
γ	0.75			R^*	1.01	κ_{ss}	0.75

B. All Equations Describing the Economy

We can summarize all the equations of the economy:

$$C_t^{-\sigma} = \beta E_t\left[C_{t+1}^{-\sigma}\frac{R_t}{\Pi_{t+1}}\right] \tag{B.1}$$

$$w_t = L_t^{\psi} C_t^{\sigma} \tag{B.2}$$

$$C_{H,t} = \gamma\frac{C_t}{p_{H,t}} \tag{B.3}$$

$$C_{F,t} = (1-\gamma)\frac{C_t}{s_t} \tag{B.4}$$

$$1 = p_{H,t}^{\gamma} s_t^{1-\gamma} \tag{B.5}$$

$$Y_t = \left(\frac{L_t}{\alpha}\right)^{\alpha}\left(\frac{Z_{t-1}}{1-\alpha}\right)^{1-\alpha} \tag{B.6}$$

$$L_t = \alpha\frac{p_{w,t}Y_t}{w_t} \tag{B.7}$$

$$n_t = (1-b_t)\, s_t Z_t \tag{B.8}$$

$$B_t = b_t Z_t \tag{B.9}$$

$$\bar{\omega}_t = \frac{R_{B,t-1}}{R^r_{Z,t}}\frac{s_t}{s_{t-1}} b_{t-1} \tag{B.10}$$

$$E_t\left[\Omega\left(\bar{\omega}_{t+1};\kappa_t\right) R^r_{Z,t+1}\frac{s_t}{s_{t+1}}\right] = R^* b_t \tag{B.11}$$

$$E_t\left[C_{t+1}^{-\sigma}\left[1-\Gamma\left(\bar{\omega}_{t+1}\right)\right] R^r_{Z,t+1}\right] = (1-b_t)\, E_t\left[C_{t+1}^{-\sigma}\frac{R_t}{\Pi_{t+1}}\right] \tag{B.12}$$

$$E_t\left[C_{t+1}^{-\sigma}\frac{R_t}{\Pi_{t+1}}\right] = E_t\left[C_{t+1}^{-\sigma}\lambda_{t+1}\frac{s_{t+1}}{s_t}R^*\right] \tag{B.13}$$

$$\lambda_t = \frac{\Gamma'\left(\bar{\omega}_t\right)}{E_t\left[\Omega'\left(\bar{\omega}_{t+1};\kappa_t\right)\right]} \tag{B.14}$$

$$R^r_{Z,t} = (1-\alpha)\frac{p_{w,t}Y_t}{s_{t-1}Z_{t-1}} \tag{B.15}$$

$$Y_t = C_{H,t} + C^*_{H,t} \tag{B.16}$$

$$C^*_{H,t} = \gamma^*\left(P^*_{H,t}\right)^{-\nu^*} C^* \tag{B.17}$$

$$F_t = C_t^{-\sigma} C_{H,t} p_{H,t}^{\eta} p_{w,t} + \alpha_p \beta E_t\left[\Pi_{t+1}^{\eta} F_{t+1}\right] \tag{B.18}$$

$$K_t = C_t^{-\sigma} C_{H,t} p_{H,t}^{\eta} + \alpha_p \beta E_t \left[\Pi_{t+1}^{\eta-1} K_{t+1} \right] \tag{B.19}$$

$$p_{H,t} = \left[(1-\alpha_p) \left(\frac{\eta}{\eta-1} \frac{F_t}{K_t} \right)^{1-\eta} + \alpha_p \left(\frac{p_{H,t-1}}{\Pi_t} \right)^{1-\eta} \right]^{\frac{1}{1-\eta}} \tag{B.20}$$

$$F_t^* = C_t^{-\sigma} C_{H,t}^* \left(P_{H,t}^* \right)^{\eta} p_{w,t} + \alpha_p \beta E_t \left[F_{t+1}^* \right] \tag{B.21}$$

$$K_t^* = C_t^{-\sigma} C_{H,t}^* \left(P_{H,t}^* \right)^{\eta} s_t + \alpha_p \beta E_t \left[K_{t+1}^* \right] \tag{B.22}$$

$$P_{H,t}^* = \left[(1-\alpha_p) \left(\frac{\eta}{\eta-1} \frac{F_t^*}{K_t^*} \right)^{1-\eta} + \alpha_p \left(P_{H,t-1}^* \right)^{1-\eta} \right]^{\frac{1}{1-\eta}} \tag{B.23}$$

$$0 = s_t P_{H,t}^* C_{H,t}^* - s_t C_{F,t} - s_t Z_t - \Gamma(\bar{\omega}_t) R_{Z,t}^r s_{t-1} Z_{t-1} + b_t s_t Z_t \tag{B.24}$$

Notice the addition of four arti.cial variables, F_t, K_t, F^*_t and K^*_t to allow for a recursive formulation of the DPI and the price of export goods.

C. Welfare Ranking

Table 4. Welfare comparison of benchmark rules

	W/W_{opt}	$\frac{W-W_{peg}}{W_{opt}-W_{peg}}$
Peg	0.788436	0
CPI stabilization	0.933456	0.685467
DPI stabilization	0.927364	0.656671
CPI Taylor	0.936369	0.699233
DPI Taylor	0.979336	0.902328
CPI dirty float	0.913253	0.589973
DPI dirty float	0.962173	0.821203

Table 5. Welfare comparison of benchmark rules under alternative scenarios

W/W_{opt}	benchmark	low nominal rigidities[1]	no nominal rigidities in exports[2]	low elast. foreign demand[3]	high elast. foreign demand[4]
Peg	0.788436	0.943950	0.749428	0.867168	0.999112
CPI stabilization	0.933456	0.885350	0.829483	0.961353	0.998578
DPI stabilization	0.927364	0.798439	0.967205	0.789743	0.986666
CPI Taylor	0.936369	0.899307	0.865398	0.969520	0.939739
DPI Taylor	0.979336	0.864994	0.950449	0.943635	0.945285
CPI dirty float	0.913253	0.915217	0.831320	0.977851	0.964824
DPI dirty float	0.962173	0.892011	0.892861	0.983912	0.963089

[1] $\alpha_p = 0.5$ in both export and domestic retail sectors
[2] $\alpha_p = 0.75$ in domestic retail sector but $\alpha_p = 0$ in export sector
[3] $\nu^* = 0.6$
[4] $\nu^* = 20$

D. Impulse Response Functions

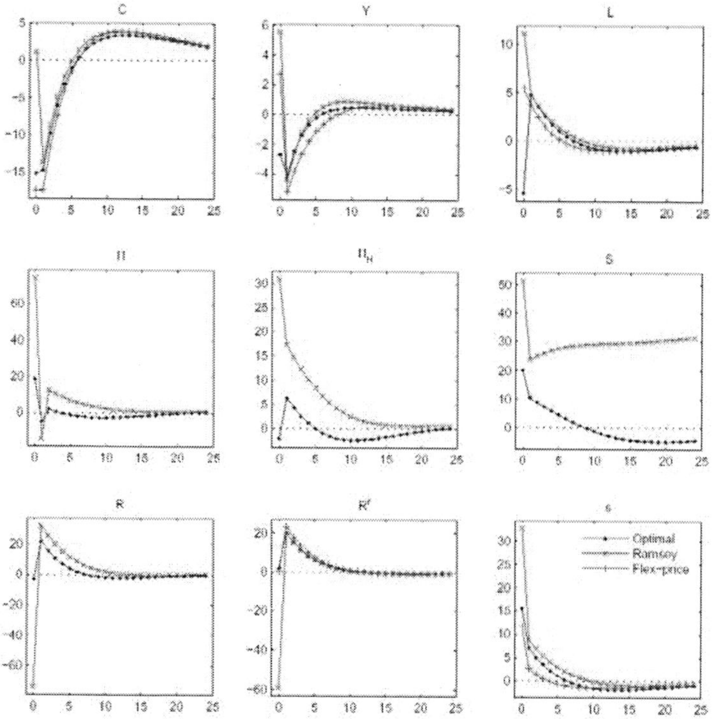

Figure 1. Responses under optimal policy.

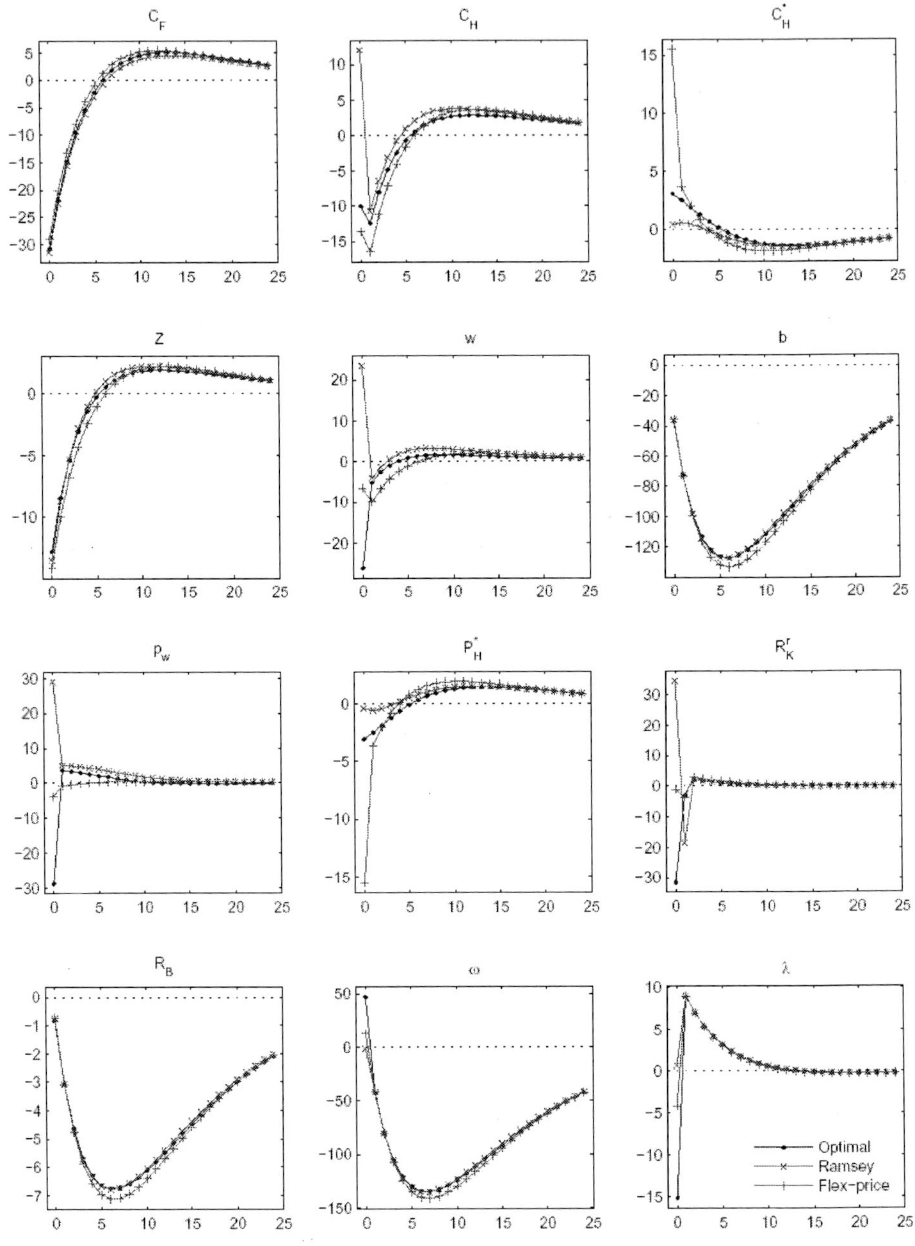

Figure 2. Responses under optimal policy (continued).

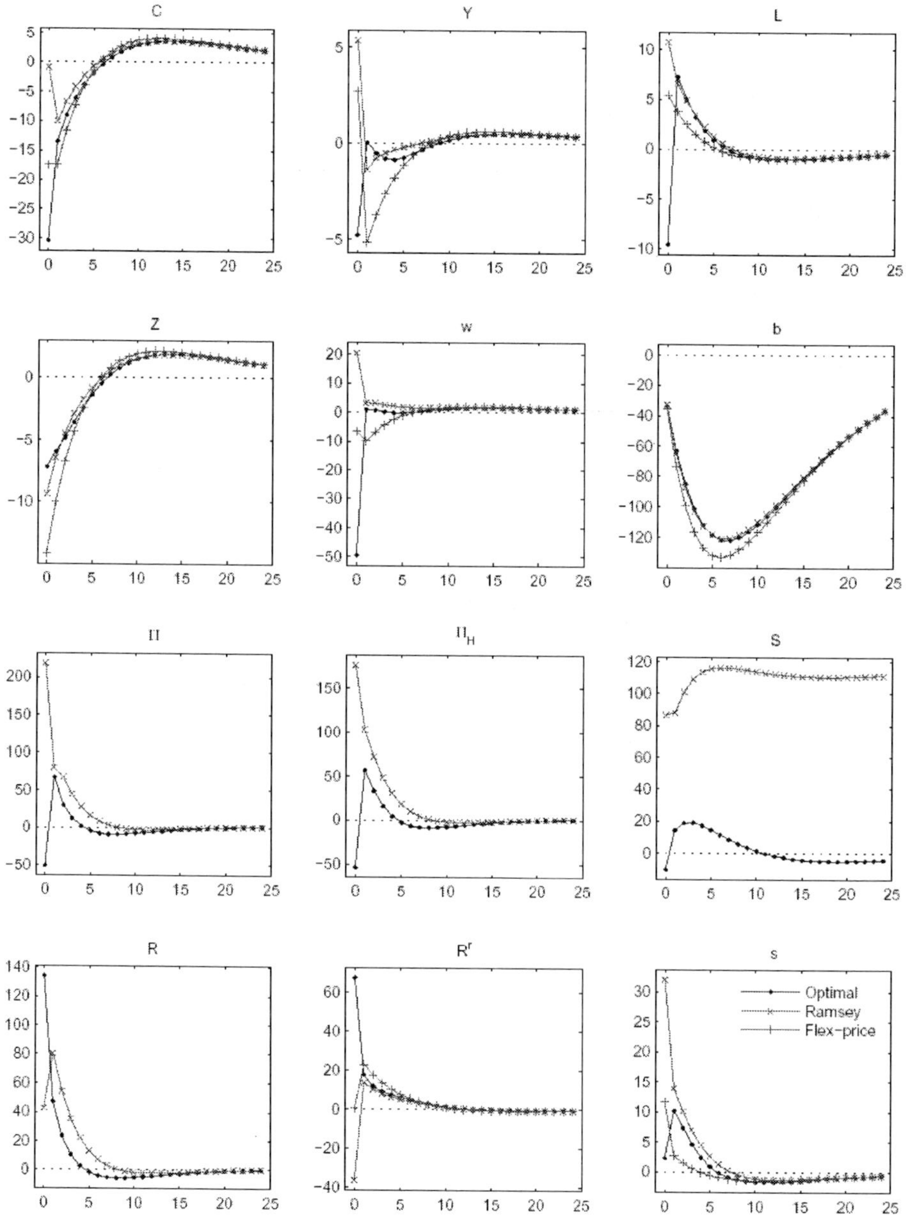

Figure 3. Responses under optimal policy with smaller nominal rigidities.

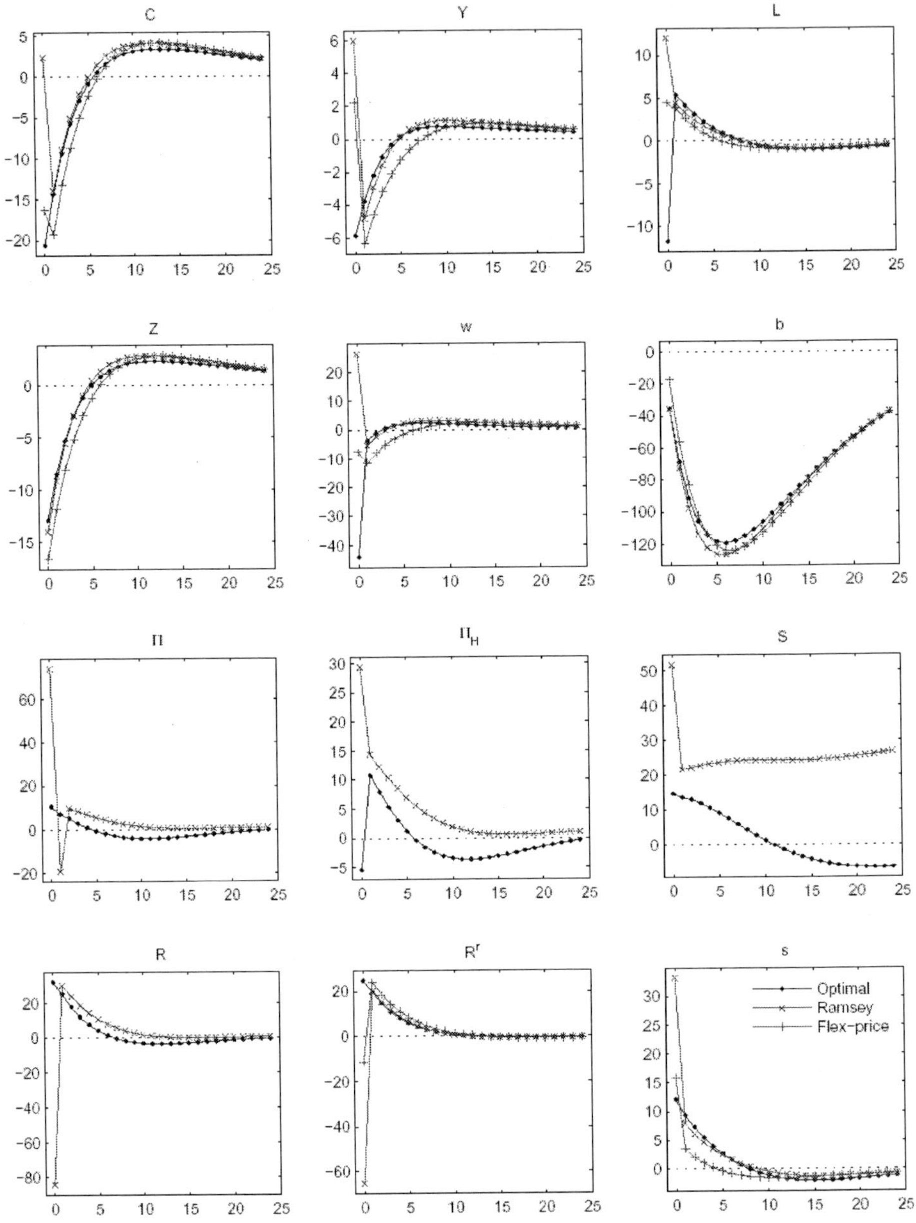

Figure 4. Responses under optimal policy with low elasticity of foreign demand.

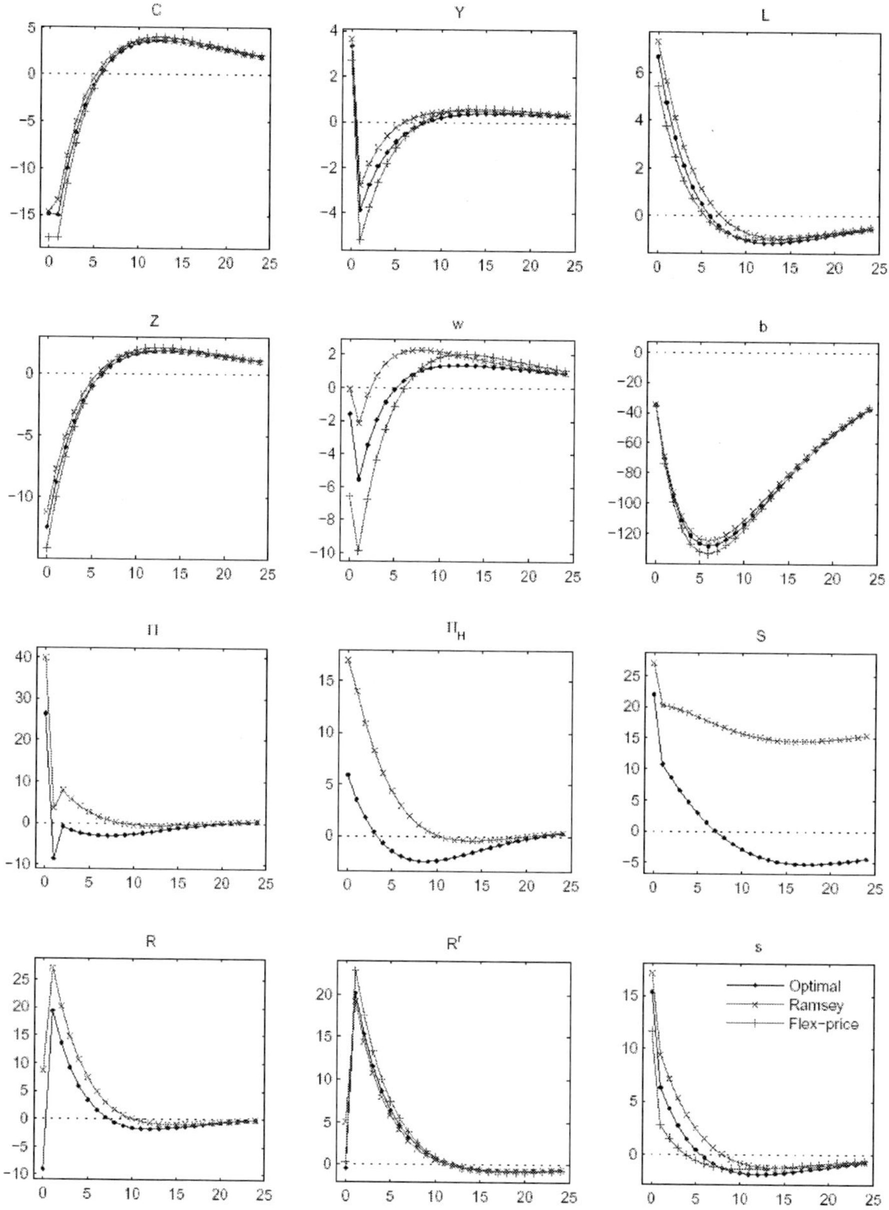

Figure 5. Responses under optimal policy without nominal rigidities in export sector.

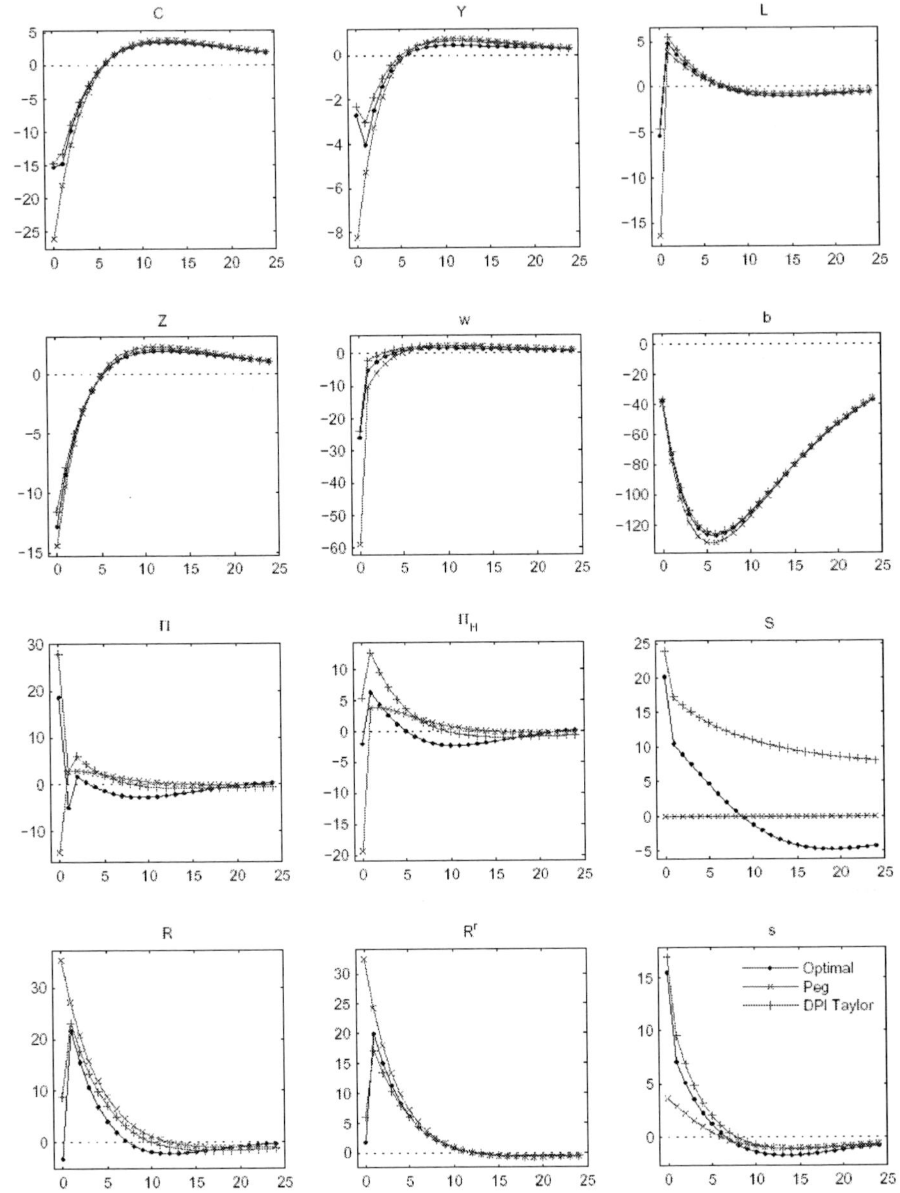

Figure 6. Responses under optimal policy and two simple rules.

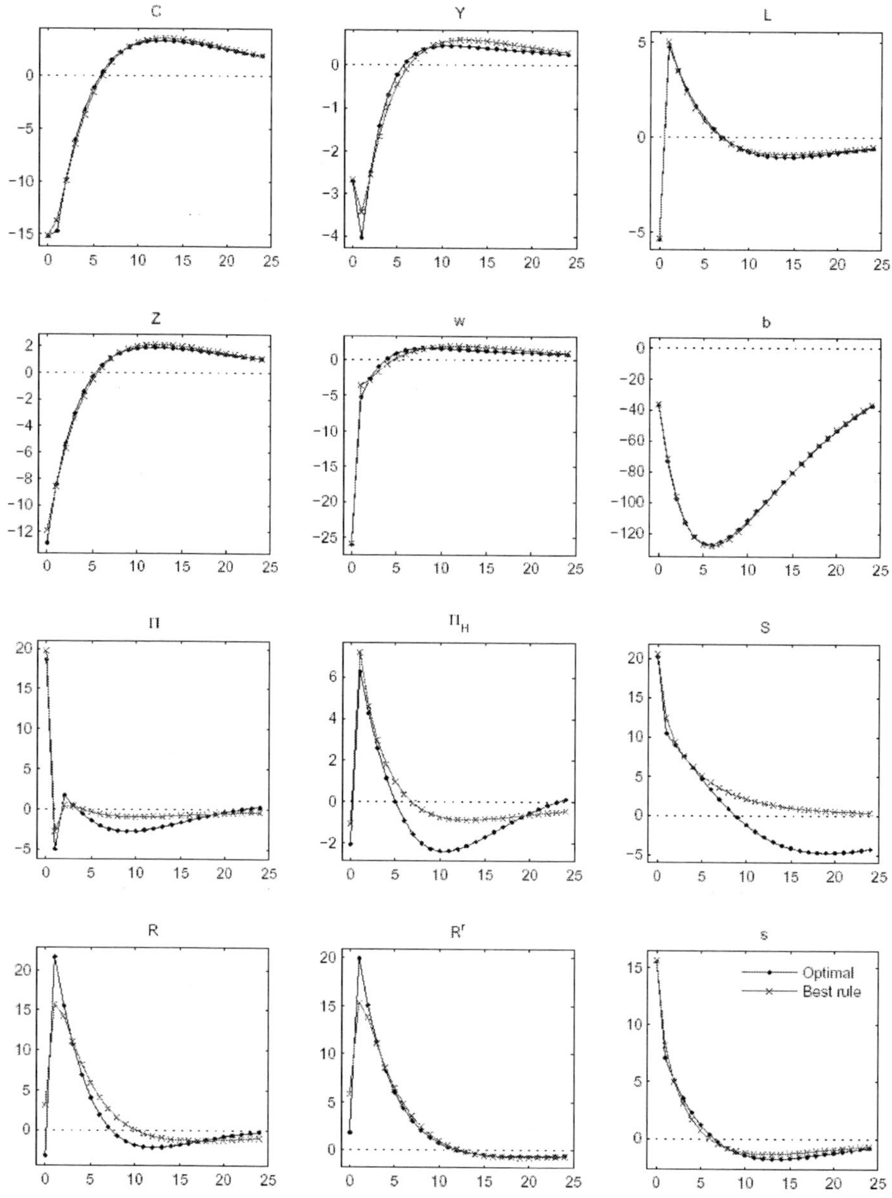

Figure 7. Responses under optimal policy and the best simple rule.

REFERENCES

Backus, D., Routledge, B., and Zin, S. (2004). Exotic preferences for macroeconomists. In Gertler, M. and Rogoff, K., editors, NBER Macroeconomics Annual 2004, chapter 5, pages 319-390. The MIT Press, Cambridge.

Benigno, P. and Woodford, M. (2006). Optimal inflation targeting under alternative fiscal regimes. *NBER Working Paper*. No. 12158.

Benigno, P. and Woodford, M. (2007). Linear-quadratic approximation of optimal policy problems. Mimeo.

Bernanke, B. and Gertler, M. (1989). Agency costs, net worth and business fluctuations. *American Economic Review,* 79(1): 14-31.

Bernanke, B. S., Gertler, M., and Gilchrist, S. (1999). The financial accelerator in a quantitative business cycle framework. In Taylor, J. B. and Woodford, M., editors, Handbook of Macroeconomics, volume 1C, chapter 21, pages 1341–93. North-Holland, Amsterdam.

Braggion, F., Christiano, L. J., and Roldos, J. (2005). Optimal monetary policy in a "sudden stop". Mimeo.

Caballero, R. J. (2001). Macroeconomic Volatility in Reformed Latin America, Diagnosis and Policy Proposals. Inter-American Development Bank, Washington, D.C.

Caballero, R. J. and Krishnamurthy, A. (2005). Inflation targeting and sudden stops. In Bernanke, B. S. and Woodford, M., editors, The Inflation-Targeting Debate, chapter 10. The University of Chicago Press, Chicago.

Calvo, G. A. (1998). Capital flows and capital-markets crises: The simple economics of sudden stops. *Journal of Applied Economics,* 1(1):35-54.

Calvo, G. A. and Reinhart, C. M. (2000). When capital inflows come to a sudden stop: Consequences and policy options. In Kenen, P. and Swoboda, A., editors, Key Issues in Reform of the International Monetary and Financial System, pages 175-20 1. International Monetary Fund, Washington DC.

Céspedes, L. F., Chang, R., and Velasco, A. (2004). Balance sheets and exchange rate policy. *American Economic Review,* 94(4): 1183-1193.

Cook, D. (2004). Monetary policy in emerging markets: Can liability dollarization explain contractionary devaluations? *Journal of Monetary Economics,* 51(6):1155–1181.

Ciirdia, V. (2007). Monetary policy under sudden stops. Federal Reserve Bank of New York Staff Report No. 278.

Devereux, M. B., Lane, P. R., and Xu, J. (2006). Exchange rates and monetary policy in emerging market economies. *The Economic Journal,* 116(511) :478-506.

Fraga, A., Goldfajn, I., and Minella, A. (2003). Inflation targeting in emerging market economies. *NBER Working Paper* No. 10019.

Gertler, M., Gilchrist, S., and Natalucci, F. M. (2003). External constraints on monetary policy and the financial accelerator. BIS Working Paper 139.

Gilboa, I. and Schmeidler, D. (1989). Maxmin expected utility with non-unique prior. *Journal of Mathematical Economics,* 18(2):141-53.

Hawkins, J. (2005). Globalisation and monetary operations in emerging economies. In Globalisation and Monetary Policy in Emerging Markets, pages 59-80. BIS Papers No 23.

Hevia, C. (2006). Optimal policy with 'sudden stops'. Mimeo.

Kydland, F. E. and Prescott, E. C. (1977). Rules rather than discretion: The inconsistency of optimal plans. *Journal of Political Economy,* 85(3):473-492.

Mishkin, F. S. (2000). Inflation targeting in emerging-market countries. American Economic Review, 90(2):105-109.

Mishkin, F. S. and Savastano, M. A. (2002). Monetary policy strategies for emerging market countries: Lessons from latin america. *Comparative Economic Studies,* 44(2/3):45-82.

Reinhart, C. M. (1994). Devaluation, relative prices, and international trade: Evidence from developing countries. *IMF Working Paper* No. 94/140.

Svensson, L. E. O. and Woodford, M. (2005). Implementing optimal policy through inflation- forecast targeting. In Bernanke, B. and Woodford, M. S., editors, The Inflation-Targeting Debate. University of Chicago Press, Chicago.

Taylor, J. B. (1993). Discretion versus policy rules in practice. Carnegie-Rochester Conference Series on Public Policy, 39:195-214.

Woodford, M. (1999). Commentary: How should monetary policy be conducted in an era of price stability? In New Challenges for Monetary Policy. Federal Reserve of Kansas City, Kansas City.

Woodford, M. (2003). Interest and Prices. Princeton University Press, Princeton.

In: Monetary Policy at the Cutting Edge
Editor: Sarah R. Porter, pp. 65-79
ISBN: 978-1-60692-321-4

Chapter 3

CURRENT ISSUES IN ECONOMICS AND FINANCIAL CYCLES

Tobias Adrian and Hyun Song Shin

A close look at how financial intermediaries manage their balance sheets suggests that these institutions raise their leverage during asset price booms and lower it during downturns— pro-cyclical actions that tend to exaggerate the fluctuations of the financial cycle. The authors of this study argue that the growth rate of aggregate balance sheets may be the most fitting measure of liquidity in a market-based financial system. Moreover, the authors show a strong correlation between balance sheet growth and the easing and tightening of monetary policy.

In recent years, financial commentators have linked stock market bubbles and housing price booms to excess liquidity in the financial system and an expansive monetary policy. However, in making these connections, the commentators often rely heavily on metaphors: "Holding interest rates too low for too long creates excess liquidity, which is now more likely to spill into the prices of homes, shares, or other assets." Or "the flood of global liquidity . . . has inflated a series of asset-price bubbles."[1] While figurative statements of this kind may be rhetorically effective, they tend to be quite imprecise, providing little insight into the economic mecha nisms underlying the linkages they describe.

[1] "Still Gushing Forth," *The Economist*, February 3, 2005; for another example, see "Bubbles Caused by Cheap Cash Menace World Economy," Reuters, July 24, 2006.

In this edition of *Current Issues*, we seek to clarify the economic relationships that exist between financial market liquidity, monetary policy, and credit cycles. Our approach is to examine how financial intermediaries react to the changes in their balance sheets that result either from market price fluctuations or from the decisions of others to increase or curtail lending and borrowing. We focus in particular on how banks adjust their leverage—defined here as the ratio of total assets to equity (net worth)—in response to a rise or fall in the value of their balance sheet assets.

Our empirical evidence suggests that banks are very aware of changes in asset value and the attendant effects on their overall leverage, and that they manage their leverage actively. More specifically, we find that institutions increase their leverage during booms and reduce it during downturns. Thus, contrary to common assumptions, financial institution leverage is *pro-cyclical*; the expansion and contraction of balance sheets amplifies, rather than counteracts, the credit cycle. A closer look at the fluctuations in balance sheets reveals that the chief tool used by institutions to adjust their leverage is collateralized borrowing and lending—in particular, repurchase agreements (repos) and reverse repurchase agreements (reverse repos), transactions in which the borrower of funds provides securities as collateral.

In line with our focus on balance sheet management, we present a new definition of liquidity as the growth rate of financial intermediaries' balance sheets. We then document how monetary policy affects overall liquidity conditions. When monetary policy is "loose" relative to macroeconomic fundamentals, financial institutions expand their balance sheets through collateralized borrowing; as a consequence, the supply of liquidity increases. Conversely, when monetary policy is "tight," institutions shrink their balance sheets, reducing the stock of repos and the overall supply of liquidity.

Our findings suggest a need to rehabilitate balance sheet quantities as a relevant measure in the conduct of monetary policy, but with one twist. Rather than reaffirming the conventional monetarist identification of the money stock as an indicator of liquidity, our analysis assigns this role to the stock of collateralized borrowing.

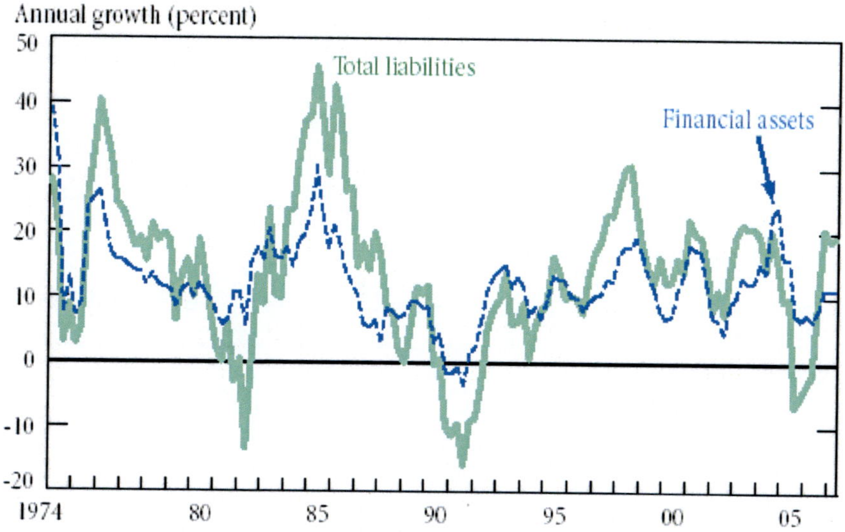

Source: Board of Governors of the Federal Reserve System, *Flow of Funds Accounts*.

Chart 1. Asset and Liability Growth of U.S. Bank Holding Companies.

ASSETS, LIABILITIES, AND THE LEVERAGE OF FINANCIAL INSTITUTIONS

To understand how banks manage their leverage, we look first at aggregate data on the assets and liabilities of U.S. bank holding companies, drawn from the Federal Reserve's *Flow of Funds Accounts* (Chart 1). As the chart shows, liabilities are more volatile than assets: during booms, banks increase their liabilities more than they increase their assets; during downturns, banks reduce their liabilities more than they reduce their assets. Thus, the overall book leverage of bank holding companies—the value of the companies' total assets divided by the value of the companies' total equity (where equity is calculated as assets minus liabilities)—rises during booms and falls during downturns, establishing a pro-cyclical pattern.

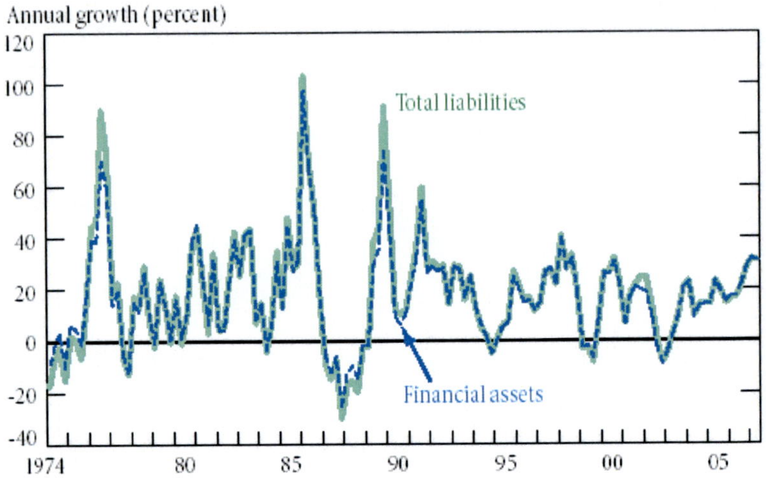

Source: Board of Governors of the Federal Reserve System, *Flow of Funds Accounts*.

Chart 2. Asset and Liability Growth of U.S. Security Brokers and Dealers.

For bank holding companies, a large proportion of assets are loans that are carried on the financial accounts at book value rather than being adjusted for the fluctuations in value that arise from changes in credit and liquidity risk over the cycle. During booms, the book value of loans will understate the market value of such loans, while during downturns in the financial cycle, the book value will overstate the loans' market value. Thus, Chart 1 is likely to exaggerate the fluctuations in leverage by failing to adjust the book value of loans to market values.

A different pattern is evident in Chart 2, which presents aggregate growth data on the assets and liabilities of security brokers and dealers (whose largest constituents are investment banks). For security brokers and dealers, assets consist largely of claims that are either marketable or very short-term in nature, such as collateralized loans. For this reason, the discrepancy between book values and market values is smaller than it is for bank holding companies.

The most striking feature of Chart 2 is that the changes in assets and liabilities appear to be very closely related. To be sure, the value of some items on the liabilities side of a security dealer's balance sheet—such as sales of borrowed securities to fund investments in other assets—might be expected to rise or fall in tandem with the value of the dealer's traded assets. However, a security dealer's liabilities consist largely of forms of short-term borrowing (for example, repurchase agreements and other types of collateralized financing) whose value would accurately reflect the current market value. Thus, the close co-movement of assets and liabilities serves as evidence of active management of leverage by the brokers and dealers themselves.

While the balance sheet data from the *Flow of Funds Accounts* are broadly suggestive, they yoke together very different financial institutions in the security broker and dealer category. To gain a more detailed understanding of financial institution behavior, we construct balance sheet data from the regulatory filings of five large U.S. investment banks.[1] The five banks are typical "stand-alone" investment banks, not owned by a large commercial banking group.

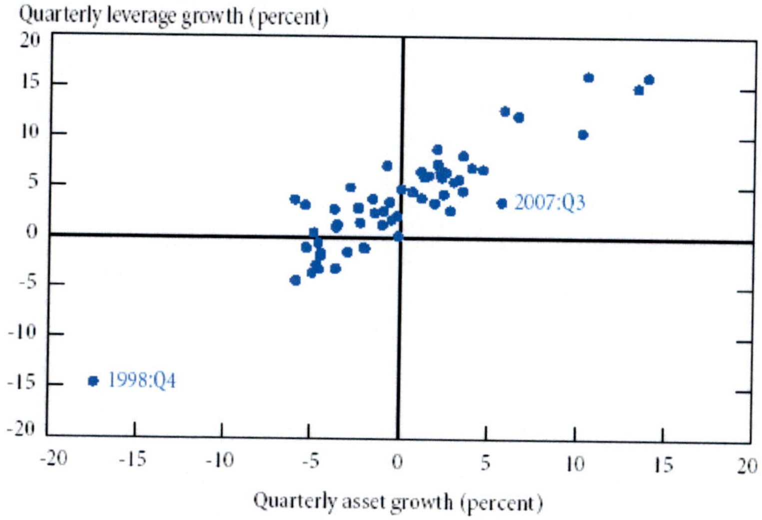

Sources: Authors' calculations; Securities and Exchange Commission, EDGAR database.

Chart 3. Total Asset Growth and Leverage Growth of U.S. Investment Banks.

Using the balance sheet data, we can plot the quarterly change in leverage for our sample of U.S. investment banks against the quarterly change in the banks' total assets (Chart 3). Given that leverage is defined as the ratio of total assets to shareholder equity, we would expect to see a negative relationship between changes in total assets and changes in leverage: That is, a rise in the value of total assets would boost equity as a proportion of total assets, leading to a decline in leverage. (By the same logic, a homeowner whose house jumped in price would be expected to experience a rise in equity and a consequent fall in leverage.)

[1] Our data source is the Securities and Exchange Commission's EDGAR database, available at <http://www.sec.gov/edgar.shtml>.

Contrary to expectations, however, Chart 3 shows a strongly positive relationship between leverage and total assets. The implication is that the investment banks are actively responding to a rise in asset value (and the consequent decline in leverage) by expanding their balance sheets.

The tool that the investment banks use to expand their balance sheets is collateralized borrowing—in particular, repurchase agreements. In these short-term borrowing transactions, the borrower of funds provides securities to the lender as collateral and agrees to repurchase the securities at a higher price on a future date. Chart 4 plots the quarterly changes in the banks' assets against the quarterly changes in repos. The two series move closely together,[1] suggesting that the banks respond to a rise in assets by taking on more liability in the form of repurchase agreements.

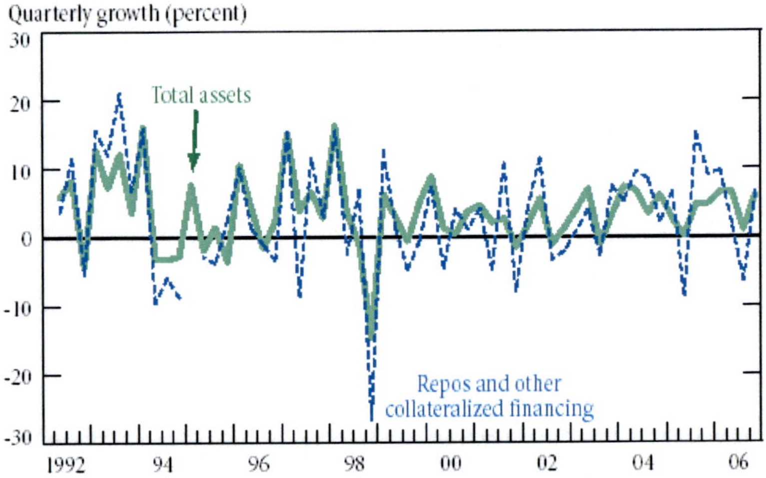

Sources: Authors' calculations; Securities and Exchange Commission, EDGAR database.

Chart 4. Total Asset Growth and Repo Growth of U.S. Investment Banks.

In sum, our evidence implies that investment bank leverage is pro-cyclical: During booms, banks increase their liabilities by more than their assets have risen, thus raising their leverage. During troughs, they reduce their liabilities more sharply than their assets have declined, thus lowering their leverage. Although the term "pro-cyclical leverage" is not one that the banks themselves would use in describing their actions, it does capture the basic nature of their practice.

---

[1] It is apparent, however, that repo growth is more volatile than the growth of total assets.

What guides the actions of the investment banks? Essentially, the banks' models of risk and economic capital dictate active management of their overall value at risk (VaR)—the risk of loss on banks' asset portfolios—through adjustments of their balance sheets. In particular, banks will adjust assets and liabilities to ensure that their total equity is proportional to the total value at risk of their assets.

Thus, for a given amount of equity, a lower value at risk allows banks to expand their balance sheets: Leverage is inversely related to value at risk. Since measured risk is countercyclical—low during booms and high during busts—the banks' efforts to control risk will lead to procyclical leverage.

From the point of view of each financial intermediary, decision rules that result in pro-cyclical leverage are readily understandable. However, in the aggregate, such behavior has consequences for the financial system as a whole that are not taken into consideration by an individual institution. In the next section, we explore these consequences by examining the economic mechanism that is set in motion by the balance sheet adjustments of financial institutions.[1]

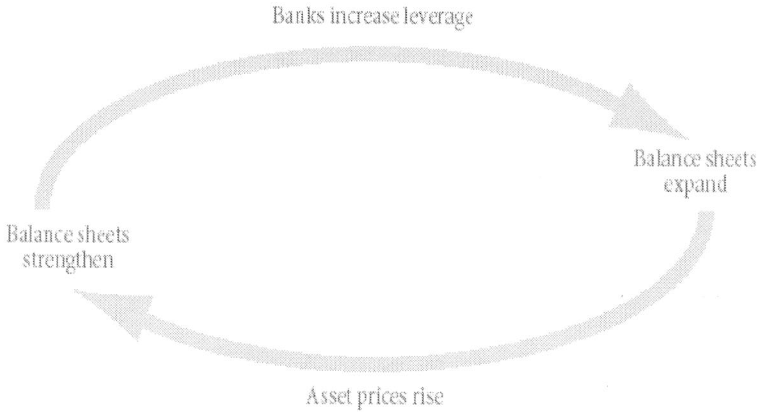

Figure 1. Leverage Management during an Asset Price Boom.

[1] Further evidence that financial institution behavior has consequences for overall financial conditions can be found in Adrian and Shin (2007). This earlier paper demonstrates that changes in collateralized borrowing by the major banks can forecast shifts in risk appetite as captured in the VIX index, a widely followed summary measure of the aversion to risk priced into the options on the S&P 500 stock index. When balance sheets expand, the VIX index tends to decline over the next week. When balance sheets contract, the VIX index tends to rise. In this sense, the fluctuations of balance sheets through collateralized borrowing can predict shifts in risk appetite.

Consequences of Pro-Cyclical Leverage

Pro-cyclical leverage offers a window on the notion of financial system liquidity. To understand how the decisions of investment banks to pursue pro-cyclical leverage affect their own balance sheets and ultimately the financial system as a whole, we look more closely at the chain of events that follows a rise in asset prices during a boom or, alternatively, a decline in asset prices during a downturn. What is evident in these sequences is that pro-cyclical leverage reverses the normal demand and supply responses to asset price changes.

Consider first a "boom" scenario in which the assets held widely by market players and intermediaries with pro-cyclical leverage increase in price. As noted earlier, this price increase will boost the equity or net worth of these institutions as a proportion of their total assets, strengthening their overall balance sheets. When balance sheets become stronger, leverage falls. Because the institutions have pro-cyclical leverage, they must respond to the erosion of leverage by raising leverage upward.

How can they restore leverage? One way is to borrow more, then use the proceeds to buy more of the assets they already hold. Such a reaction—buying more, rather than less, of an asset when its price is rising—clearly reverses the normal demand response.

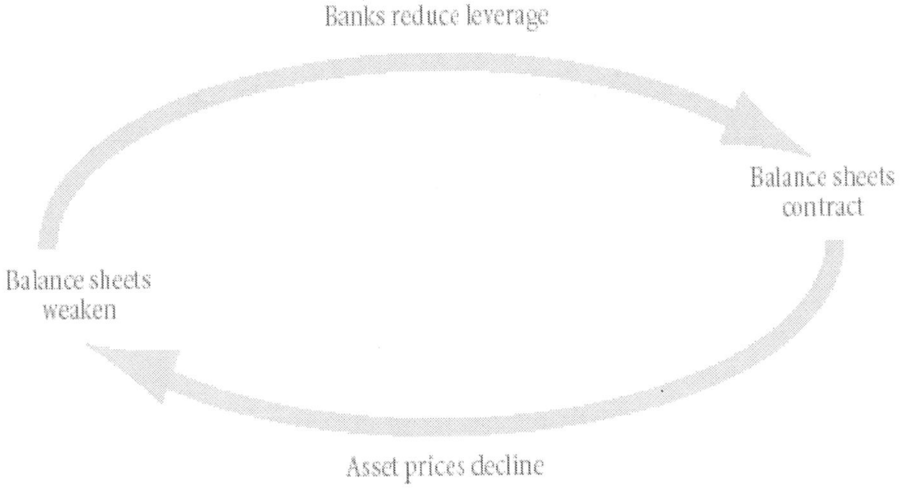

Figure 2. Leverage Management during an Asset Price Decline.

If, moreover, increased demand for the asset tends to put upward pressure on its price, there is the potential for a feedback effect: the stronger balance sheets lead to greater demand for the asset, and this outcome in turn raises the asset's price and further strengthens the balance sheets. Having come full circle, the feedback process goes through another turn (Figure 1).

During downturns, the mechanism works in reverse. Consider a scenario in which asset prices decline. Then, the net worth of institutions will fall faster than the rate at which their assets decrease in value. As the institutions' balance sheets weaken, their leverage will increase. Since these institutions are targeting pro-cyclical leverage, however, they must attempt to reduce leverage in some way—in some cases, quite drastically.

How do these institutions reduce leverage? One way is to sell some assets, then use the proceeds to pay down debt. Thus, a fall in the price of the asset can lead to an increase in the supply of the asset, overturning the normal supply response to a drop in asset price.

If we further hypothesize that greater supply of the asset tends to put downward pressure on its price, then there is again the potential for a feedback effect. Weaker balance sheets lead to greater sales of the asset, and this outcome in turn depresses the asset's price and leads to even weaker balance sheets. But weaker balance sheets will kick off another cycle of selling and price declines (Figure 2).

Of course, the perverse nature of the demand and supply responses applies solely to leveraged institutions. Nonleveraged institutions—such as households, pension funds, and insurance companies—can be expected to moderate the amplification mechanism created by the balance sheet dynamics. How fully they can offset this mechanism remains unclear, however.

A NEW DEFINITION OF LIQUIDITY

Our discussion of financial institution behavior suggests a natural definition of liquidity as the *rate of growth of aggregate balance sheets*. In more concrete terms, we can define liquidity as the rate of growth of repos, since repos and other forms of collateralized borrowing are the tool that financial institutions use to adjust their balance sheets.

When financial intermediaries' balance sheets are generally strong, their leverage is low. They hold surplus capital, and will attempt to find ways in which they can employ it. In an analogy with manufacturing firms, the financial system could be said to have "surplus capacity." For such surplus capacity to be utilized, the intermediaries must expand their balance sheets. On the liabilities side, they take on more short-term debt. On the asset side, they search for potential borrowers to lend to. Aggregate liquidity, we suggest, is intimately tied to how hard the financial intermediaries search for borrowers. In the case of the subprime mortgage market in the United States, we have seen that when balance sheets are expanding fast enough, even borrowers who do not have the means to repay are granted credit—so intense is the urge to employ surplus capital. In this way, the conditions are set for the subsequent downturn in the credit cycle.

The Role of Money

In what sense is our notion of aggregate liquidity related to the traditional notion of liquidity as the money stock? In a hypothetical world where deposit-taking banks are the only financial intermediaries and where their liabilities (deposits) can be identified with a broad definition of "money," the money stock would be a good indicator of the aggregate size of the balance sheets of leveraged institutions. To this extent, the growth of the money stock would play a useful role in signaling changes in the size of the aggregate balance sheet of the leveraged sector.

However, it is clear that we cannot readily identify money with the aggregate size of the liabilities of leveraged institutions. First, many of the leveraged institutions—investment banks, hedge funds, off-balance-sheet vehicles and others— do not conform to the textbook ideal of the deposit-funded bank. Hence, their liabilities are not counted as money. Second, even for banks that are mainly deposit-funded, not all liabilities qualify as money. The banks also raise funding from financial markets to supplement their deposit funding.

Just as the money stock is a poor measure of aggregate liquidity, so excessive growth of the money stock is a flawed measure of excess liquidity. To be sure, if the financial system were dominated by deposit-taking banks, so that the aggregate liabilities of the financial system as a whole were well captured by the stock of deposits, then excess liquidity would correspond to excessive growth of the money stock. Deposits fall under conventional broad notions of money. However, the ideal of a financial system dominated by deposit-funded banks may never have existed in its purest form, and it is becoming less relevant over time. Certainly, empirical evidence from the United States since the 1980s detects very little role for the money stock in explaining macroeconomic fluctuations (see, for example, Friedman [1988]).

If the financial system is instead organized around the capital market, then conventional measures of money represent only a small proportion of the aggregate size of the leveraged sector. Nor is the quantity of deposits the most volatile component of the total aggregate liabilities of the financial system. In such a world, money is less useful as a measure of liquidity. The rapid move toward a market-based financial system in recent years has accelerated the trend toward greater reliance on nontraditional, non-deposit-based funding and toward greater use of the interbank market, the market for commercial paper, and asset-backed securities.

Liquidity and Monetary Policy

The concept of liquidity we proposed earlier—the growth rate of aggregate balance sheets or, more precisely, the growth rate of outstanding repurchase agreements—is a far better measure for a modern, market-based financial system than is the money stock. In this section, we focus on the question whether our preferred notion of liquidity has any bearing on monetary policy, and in particular whether the growth of repos is linked in a direct way with the easing or tightening of monetary policy.

Our empirical tests of this relationship suggest that the answer to this question is a resounding "yes." We find that repo growth is closely correlated with the ease or restrictiveness of monetary policy as measured by the Taylor rule (see the box). The Taylor rule specifies how a central bank should alter its targeted short-term interest rate (the federal funds rate in the United States) in response to evolving macroeconomic fundamentals—specifically, the divergence of current output from potential output and of current inflation from the desired rate of inflation. We show that when monetary policy is loose in the sense that the federal funds rate is lower than the rate implied by the Taylor rule, there is rapid growth in repos and financial market liquidity is high. Conversely, when monetary policy is tight in the sense that the fed funds rate is higher than the rate implied by the Taylor rule, repo growth is much lower, even negative at times, and financial market liquidity is low.[1]

THE LINK BETWEEN MONETARY POLICY AND THE GROWTH OF REPOS

To test the relationship between monetary policy and the growth of repurchase agreements, we estimate the following Taylor rule:

Federal funds target = 1.3 + 0.8 X output gap
+1.3 X inflation rate + Taylor rule residual.

We calculate the output gap as the percentage difference between real (inflation-adjusted) GDP and real potential GDP, and the inflation rate as the annual percentage growth of the core consumer price index (core CPI). Summary statistics for these variables, as well as the Taylor rule residual from the equation, are given in Table A1. All coefficients in the equation are statistically significant at the 1 percent level.

Following Taylor (1993), we can interpret the predicted value from the equation as "rule-based" monetary policy, and the Taylor rule residual as "discretionary" monetary policy. A positive residual indicates tight monetary policy relative to the rule, while a negative residual indicates relatively loose policy. The R2 of the equation is 75 percent, indicating that three quarters of the variation in monetary policy is attributable to the Taylor rule, while one quarter of the variation is discretionary.

As a measure of aggregate growth of repurchase agreement liabilities, we use the comprehensive figures for the socalled primary dealers that have a trading relationship with the Federal Reserve Bank of New York (see Adrian and Fleming [2005] and Kambhu [2006] for earlier analysis of the primary dealer repo data). One advantage of these data is that they include the marked-to-market repo financing of investment banks, commercial banks with large investment banking operations, and nonbank security brokers and dealers. The primary dealer data can thus be interpreted as an aggregate measure of the financial system's repo financing. Our key results relating repo growth to the stance of monetary policy are contained in Table A2.

[1] For a discussion of these relationships from a policymaker's perspective, see Tucker (2007).

Table A1. Summary Statistics for Taylor Rule Regressions 1991:Q3 to 2007:Q1

	Mean	Standard Deviation	Minimum	Maximum
Primary dealer repo growth	14.32	11.03	-17.69	34.92
Outstanding financial commercial paper growth	10.07	10.38	-5.49	29.24
Federal funds target rate	4.07	1.67	1.00	6.50
Output gap	-0.72	1.60	-3.18	2.91
Core CPI inflation	2.56	0.65	1.15	4.60
Taylor rule residuals	0.00	0.95	-1.81	2.40

Sources: Board of Governors of the Federal Reserve System, H.15 statistical releases, for data on growth in outstanding commercial paper; Federal Reserve Bank of New York, for primary dealer statistics and the federal funds target rate; U.S. Con gressional Budget Office, for the output gap; U.S. Department of Labor, for core CPI inflation; authors' calculations.

Notes: All growth rates are annual percentages. Primary dealer repo growth is the annual growth rate of the repurchase agreement liabilities of the Federal Reserve's primary dealers. The output gap is the percentage difference between current real GDP and potential real GDP. Taylor rule residuals are the residuals of an ordinary least squares regression of the federal funds target rate on core CPI inflation and the output gap.

When the residuals of the Taylor rule regression are negative (that is, when the federal funds rate is lower than that predicted by the Taylor rule), repo growth is higher than average. Conversely, when the residuals of the Taylor rule regression are positive (that is, when the fed funds rate is higher than that predicted by the Taylor rule), repo growth is lower than average, sometimes even becoming negative.

Interestingly, the behavior of repos is quite different from that of commercial paper. Although both repos and commercial paper are forms of short-term borrowing, the evidence suggests that financial intermediaries take on more of one when the other is less available. The coefficients on the liquidity regression using commercial paper growth instead of repo growth (reported in columns 3 and 4 of Table A2) show signs exactly opposite to those for repo growth. One possible explanation for the reverse in signs could be that financial intermediaries turn to commercial paper when repos are difficult to obtain (for example, during the hedge fund crisis of 1998). Conversely, when repos are increasing rapidly so that balance sheet capacity is low, there is less spare capacity for the issuance of commercial paper. The credit crisis of 2007 conforms to the latter scenario.

Table A2. Taylor Rule Regressions 1991:Q3 to 2007:Q1

	Primary Dealer Repo Growth		Financial Commercial Paper Growth	
	(1)	(2)	(3)	(4)
Fed funds target	-2.29**		4.77***	
Taylor rule residuals		-4.68***		5.61***
Taylor rule fed funds prediction		-1.11		5.49***
Constant	23.64***	18.85***	-9.35***	-7.89***
R^2 (percent)	12	18	59	59

Source: Authors' calculations.

Note: This table reports regressions of primary dealer repo growth rates and outstanding commercial paper growth rates on the federal funds target rate and Taylor rule residuals.

** Significant at the 5 percent level.

*** Significant at the 1 percent level.

CONCLUSION

Our look at how banks and other financial intermediaries manage their balance sheets reveals that these institutions increase their leverage during asset price booms and reduce it during busts. This pro-cyclical behavior is likely to exacerbate financial market fluctuations as institutions overturn the normal supply and demand responses by buying assets when the price rises and selling them when the price falls.

These findings lead us to propose a new definition of financial market liquidity as the growth rate of aggregate balance sheets—or, more specifically, as the growth rate of repurchase agreements, the tool used by financial institutions to adjust their leverage.

Taking our analysis a step further, we show that the growth rate of repos is closely related to the degree of ease in monetary policy: when monetary policy is loose, the stock of repos grows rapidly and market liquidity is high; when monetary policy is tight, repo growth is slow and market liquidity declines markedly. One implication of the link between repo growth and monetary policy is that the short-term rate targeted by policymakers (the federal funds rate in the United States) may be a key price variable in its own right. This rate has been regarded mainly as a vehicle for signaling the central bank's intentions to the financial markets and thereby influencing the markets' expectations about the future course of central bank actions. In contrast to this orthodox view, our results suggest that the policy rate—through its effects on the cost of leverage—may be an important determinant of the expansion and contraction of balance sheets and the liquidity of the financial system. Certainly, the financial turmoil of 2007 has dramatically underscored the significance of financial intermediaries' balance sheets for market performance and hence for monetary policy. Financial system liquidity emerges as the crucial concept that ties balance sheet management, asset prices, and monetary policy together.

REFERENCES

Adrian, Tobias, and Michael J. Fleming. 2005. "What Financing Data Reveal about

Dealer Leverage." Federal Reserve Bank of New York. *Current Issues in Economics and Finance.* 11, no. 3 (March).

Adrian, Tobias, and Hyun Song Shin. 2007. "Liquidity and Leverage." Paper presented at the Bank for International Settlements conference "Financial System and Macroeconomic Resilience," Brunnen, Switzerland, June 18. Available at <http://www.princeton.edu/~hsshin/www/ LiquidityLeverage .pdf>.

Friedman, Benjamin M. 1988. "Monetary Policy without Quantity Variables." *American Economic Review* 78, no. 2 (May): 440-5. Papers and Proceedings of the 100th Annual Meeting of the American Economic Association.

Kambhu, John. 2006. "Trading Risk, Market Liquidity, and Convergence Trading in the Interest Rate Swap Spread." Federal Reserve Bank of New York *Economic Policy Review* 12, no. 1 (May): 1-13.

Taylor, John B. 1993. "Discretion versus Policy Rules in Practice." *Carnegie-Rochester Conference Series on Public Policy* 39: 195-214.

Tucker, Paul. 2007. "Money and Credit: Banking and the Macroeconomy." Speech delivered at the conference "Monetary Policy and the Markets," London, December 13. Available at <http://www.bankofengland.co.uk/ publications/speeches/2007/speech331.pdf>.

In: Monetary Policy at the Cutting Edge
Editor: Sarah R. Porter, pp. 81-98

ISBN: 978-1-60692-321-4

Chapter 4

DOLLAR CRISIS: PROSPECT AND IMPLICATIONS*

Craig K. Elwell

ABSTRACT

The dollar's value in international exchange has been falling since early 2002. Over this five year span, the currency, on a real trade weighted basis, is down about 29%. For most of this time the dollar's fall was moderately paced at about 3.0% to 4.0% annually. Recently, however, the slide has accelerated, falling nearly 10% between January and December of 2007. An acceleration of the depreciation brings the periodic concern of an impending dollar crisis to the fore. There is no precise demarcation of when a falling dollar moves from being an orderly decline to being a crisis. Most likely it would be a situation where the dollar falls, perhaps 15% to 20% annually for several years, and sends a significant negative shock to the U.S. and the global economies. This crisis may not be an inevitable outcome, but one that likely presents considerable risk to the economy.

The large U.S. current account deficits are sustained by an inflow of foreign capital. That inflow also exerts upward pressure on the value of the dollar as investors demand dollars to enable the purchase of dollar denominated assets. There is a limit to how much external debt even the U.S. economy can incur. Erasing the U.S. trade gap would stop the accumulation of debt. This would occur through a rebalancing of global spending, composed of a

---

* Excerpted from CRS Report RL34311, dated January 8, 2008.

decrease of domestic spending in the United States and an increase of domestic spending in the surplus economies. Such shifts in domestic spending patterns must be induced by a depreciation of the dollar, causing the price of foreign goods to rise for U.S. buyers and the price of U.S. goods to fall for foreign buyers.

The critical factor governing whether orderly and disorderly adjustment of international imbalances occurs is foreign investor expectations about future dollar depreciation. Rational expectations will have a smoothing effect on the size of international capital flows. In contrast, a sharp plunge of the dollar is likely to occur if investors do not form rational expectations. If the dollar then depreciates at a rate faster than foreign investors now expect, a dollar crisis becomes likely. Currently foreign investors do not appear to have a realistic expectation of future dollar depreciation. A dollar crisis could start when they realize their error and try to move quickly out of dollar assets — the likely stampede would cause a "dollar crisis." Three prominent counter-arguments to the dollar crisis prediction (the *global savings glut* argument, the *Bretton Woods II* argument, and the *economic dark matter* argument) do not offer credible alternatives to the dollar crisis outcome.

The transition to a new equilibrium of trade balances may not be smooth, likely involving a slowdown in economic activity or a recession. The ongoing U.S. housing price crisis raises the risk of a dollar crisis causing a recession. With fiscal policy most likely out of consideration in the near term, the task of attempting to counter the short-term contractionary effects of a dollar crisis would fall upon the Federal Reserve. A stimulative monetary policy can be implemented quickly but its eventual effectiveness is uncertain. The most useful policy response by foreign economies would be complementary expansionary policies to offset the negative impact of their appreciating currencies on their net exports. Attempts to defend a currency against this crisis driven appreciation would be costly and likely fail.

INTRODUCTION

The dollar's value in international exchange has been falling since early 2002. Over this five-year span, the currency, on a real trade-weighted basis, is down about 29%.[1] This depreciation has been orderly so far. For most of this, time the dollar's fall was moderately paced at about 3.0% to 4.0% annually. Recently, however, the slide has accelerated, falling nearly 10% between January and November of 2007, but falling faster over the last four months than during the previous seven months.

An acceleration of the depreciation brings the periodic concern of an impending dollar crisis to the fore. There is no precise demarcation of when a falling dollar moves from being an orderly decline to being a crisis. Most likely it would be a situation where the dollar falls, perhaps 15% to 20% annually for several years, and sends a significant negative shock to the U.S. and the global economies. This crisis may not be an inevitable outcome, but one that likely presents considerable risk.

That negative shock will likely lead to some degree of slowing of economic activity. For the U.S. economy, already weakened by the ongoing housing price crisis, a further dampening effect caused by a plummeting dollar would significantly raise the risk of recession. For the rest of the world, the impact would also depend on what else was going on in their economies at the time of the dollar's fall. It is likely that the negative impact would be substantial for foreign economies that are highly dependent on export sales to the United States.[2]

This concern about the dollar's near-term path raises three questions: (1) will a dollar crisis occur? (2) what macroeconomic impact might a dollar crisis have on U.S. economy, and the world economy? and (3) are there policy responses that can counter adverse impacts?

ANATOMY OF DOLLAR CRISIS

The large U.S. current account deficits are sustained by an inflow of foreign capital. The necessary counterpart for this inflow to occur is economies in the rest of the world that generate capital outflows and run trade surpluses. The country with a trade deficit is an international borrower and is accumulating external liabilities. The economies with trade surpluses are international lenders and accumulate external assets.

The capital inflow to the United States also exerts upward pressure on the value of the dollar as investors demand dollars to purchase dollar denominated assets. The upward demand pressure on the value of the dollar is pulling against the downward pressure on the dollar exerted by the large supply of dollars pumped into the foreign exchange markets by the U.S. trade deficit. From the mid-1990s until early 2002, the strength of foreign demand for dollar assets was sufficient to keep the dollar appreciating despite the rapid expansion of the trade deficit in this time period. Since 2002, however, although the United States continued to receive a rising inflow of capital, the strength of the associated demand for dollars has not been sufficient to prevent the dollar from depreciating moderately under the weight of large current account deficits in this time period.[3]

This external financing of the U.S. current account deficit has occurred with relative ease so far. But large scale borrowing can not go on indefinitely. There is a limit to how much external debt even the U.S. economy can incur. Currently, the U.S. debt/GNP ratio is at a historical high of about 22%. It is uncertain how much higher this ratio can go, but most economists would argue that there is an upper bound and at some point the US. trade deficit will need to be closed to stabilize the level of external debt at a feasible level.

Erasing the U.S. trade gap will require a rebalancing of global spending. A trade deficit is a symptom of an economy that spends more than it produces; therefore, rebalancing requires a decrease of domestic spending in the United States. In contrast, a trade surplus is a symptom of an economy that spends less than it produces; therefore, rebalancing requires an increase of domestic spending in surplus economies. These shifts in domestic spending patterns can be induced by a decrease in the price of U.S. goods and services relative to the price of foreign goods and services. For the change in relative prices to happen the dollar must fall, causing the price of foreign goods to rise for U.S. buyers and the price of U.S. goods to fall for foreign buyers. In addition to the downward pressure on the dollar of the large trade deficit, an important animating force in this adjustment would likely be a reduction in the demand for dollar denominated assets by foreign investors and a shrinking of the associated capital inflow.

This rebalancing of global spending does not have to be disorderly and disruptive. The major depreciation of the dollar that followed the breakup of the Bretton Woods international monetary system in the early 1 970s was largely orderly. More recently, the protracted fall of the dollar and reduction of the U.S. trade deficit in the late 1980s and early 1990s was also an orderly adjustment of international economic imbalances.

Why might a disorderly adjustment and dollar crisis occur? The critical factor is foreign investor expectations about future dollar depreciation. Economic theory indicates that a rational foreign investor in deciding whether to hold more or continue to hold his current dollar assets will build into that decision some estimate of future dollar deprecation. For example, a dollar asset and a euro asset each of similar risk and each offering a 2% real return would present very different *expected* returns if the dollar is expected to depreciate 4% annually and the euro to remain steady over the holding period. With these expectations, the rational investor would need the dollar asset to offer a real yield in excess of 6% to make it more attractive then the euro asset at 2%.

A moderation of market behavior and crisis free adjustment occurs when foreign investors develop rational expectations about the currency's future path. Rational expectations about the dollar's future path will have a smoothing effect on the size of international capital flows. In a time of capital inflows, some expectation of possible future depreciation tends to moderate those inflows. Conversely, in a time of capital outflows, some expectation of possible future appreciation will tend to moderate those outflows.

In contrast, a sharp plunge of the dollar is likely to occur if investors do not form rational expectations about the dollar's future path. If the dollar then depreciates at a rate faster than foreign investors now expect, a dollar crisis becomes likely. The rate of depreciation of the dollar that is rational to expect is the rate which is consistent with avoiding the accumulation of an unsustainable level of U.S. external debt. It is, however, difficult to say what that debt level is. Nevertheless, there is a debt/GDP ratio that prudent economic agents will judge to be an upper bound. Given that, the question becomes: what rate of dollar depreciation will give a rate of closure of the trade deficit that contains the debt/GDP ratio below that upper bound?

The economist Paul Krugman has calculated a range of estimates of U.S. external debt accumulation under alternative rates of convergence of the trade deficit to balance.[4] He assumes, based on the general consensus of experts, that a further real depreciation of the dollar of about 35% would, at a minimum, be necessary to close the U.S. trade gap.[5] He then considers two rates of convergence to this goal: one occurring over 20 years with a 1.75% annual rate of depreciation of the dollar. It leads to an external debt/ GDP ratio of 118%. At that size it is possible that a third or more of the U.S. capital stock would be foreign owned. The second scenario has convergence occurring over 10 years with an annual rate of depreciation of the dollar of about 3.75%. It leads to an external debt/GDP ratio of 58%, which is more than twice the size of the current historically high level of U.S. debt/GDP ratio. That seems high for a large, relatively closed economy like the United States, but, perhaps, plausible given the current trends in financial globalization.

Guarding against an overly pessimistic outcome, these computations incorporate significant constraints on the growth of the external dept/GDP ratio. For instance, each estimate of the eventual debt to GDP ratio assumes that nominal GDP will grow at an annual rate of 5.5%, with a combination of 3.0% real GDP growth and 2.5% inflation rate. This could be a slightly optimistic assumption for the pace of real GDP growth, which has averaged only 2.7% in the current economic expansion. Slower growth of GDP would make the Debt/GDP ratio climb faster.

Also, Krugman's external debt estimates take into account the tendency of a depreciating dollar to improve the U.S. net debt position. This improvement is caused by favorable valuation effects on U.S. foreign assets. These occur because U.S. foreign liabilities are largely denominated in dollars, but U.S. foreign assets are largely denominated in foreign currencies. Therefore, a real depreciation of the dollar increases the value of U.S. external assets and largely does not increase the value of U.S. external liabilities. This asymmetry in the currency composition of U.S. external assets and liabilities results in a dollar depreciation reducing U.S. net external debt.[6]

Exchange rate induced valuation effects are substantial because they apply to the entire stock of U.S. foreign assets, valued at near $14 trillion in 2006. The large scale of U.S. foreign assets means that valuation changes can offset a sizable portion of the current account's deficits annual addition to the existing stock of external debt. For example, in 2006, the current account deficit made a $811.4 billion contribution to U.S. external debt. But the total value of net external debt in 2006 increased only about $300 billion due to an offset of over $500 billion (over 60%); nearly half of this offset was attributable to positive valuation effects on U.S. foreign assets caused by the dollars depreciation that year.[7] If rapid dollar depreciation causes significant numbers of future lenders to be only willing to hold non dollar denominated U.S. debt the scale of the positive valuation effects would shrink and make the debt/GDP ratio climb faster.

In addition, one could argue that the 35% real depreciation target understates what is needed to close the current account deficit. For the United States, the equilibrium exchange rate is probably a moving target, and one whose path has been uneven but on balance has fallen over the past 30 years. This secular decline is thought to be rooted in rising technology in emerging economies that has allowed them to generate a steady rise in exports that compete with U.S. tradable goods. It is difficult to predict the pace of this secular decline, but during the 10- to 20-year convergence period used in this analysis, it is possible that reaching the equilibrium exchange rate will require more than the exercise's assumed 35% real depreciation of the dollar.

Taken together, these considerations probably give Krugman' s computations of the implied rise of the debt/GNP ratios a bias toward understatement. Nevertheless, the scale of the U.S. trade imbalance that needs to be eliminated causes the estimated ratio to soar in either alternative. If these estimates are understated, then even more rapid real depreciation would be needed to erase the trade deficit and keep the debt to GNP ratio below a realistic upper bound.

Based on these computations, Krugman argues that a rational foreign investor would have to expect the dollar to depreciate by, at least, about 2% per year and very likely depreciate by 4% per year or more. Do holders of U.S. assets appear to have taken this probable depreciation into account? It appears they have not. Using estimates of real long-term interest rates in the United States, the euro area, and Japan, Krugman finds no difference in real yield between the U.S. and euro area assets, and about a 1 percentage point advantage for U.S. assets over Japan's assets.

This lack of a real interest rate spread between dollar assets and similar foreign assets indicates that investors are expecting virtually no depreciation of the dollar over the holding period. Therefore, in the face of a seemingly inevitable depreciation of the dollar at 2% or faster, these investors are holding U.S. assets that offer, in terms of their own currency, a zero or negative real return.

When foreign investors come to realize their error and try to avoid large capital loses by moving quickly and substantially out of dollar assets, the dollar will fall precipitously and the dollar crisis begins. As the dollar's fall gains momentum there are likely to be negative interactions with domestic financial markets and domestic economic activity that will add to this downward momentum, overcoming, for awhile, the usual corrective mechanisms.

In a dollar crisis, it is unlikely that the current account deficit could decrease as rapidly as foreign investors would desire to curtail the inflow of capital to the United States. But the current account deficit will have to be financed. This economic necessity will generate strong economic forces to assure that the needed economic adjustments, at home and abroad, occur. The necessary macroeconomic adjustments will be discussed in a subsequent section of the report. At this point it will be useful to consider possible counter arguments to a dollar crisis happening.

Possible Reasons Why a Dollar Crisis Won't Occur

Over the last few years, several arguments that offer reasons why the U.S.trade deficit is more sustainable and a dollar crisis less likely than presented in Krugman's analysis have received serious consideration in policy discussions about the U.S. trade deficit and the associated rise of U.S. external debt. This section evaluates three prominent counterarguments to the dollar crisis prediction: the *global savings glut* argument, the *Bretton Woods II* argument, and the *economic dark matter* argument.[8]

Global Savings Glut

Ben Bernanke, now chairman of the Federal Reserve Board, has argued that there exists outside of the United States a large excess of global saving relative to global investment opportunities.[9] These large and growing flows of foreign saving are the result of the rapid economic growth of many emerging economies and large oil earnings by petroleum exporting countries. A large share of these funds are not going to be used in the home economy and are attracted to U.S.

asset markets because they offer excellent wealth storage services. This service encompasses the ability of U.S. asset markets to offer a combination of reasonable rates of return, safety, and high liquidity. The result has been unusually large capital inflows to the United States.

These inflows of capital have kept U.S. interest rates low and have exerted strong upward pressure on the value of dollar. It is argued that this saving glut could continue to grow for many years into the future. Therefore, it will continue to enhance the sustainability of the U.S. trade deficit and, in turn, provides sustained and substantial upward pressure on the value of the dollar. This persisting inflow does not preclude depreciation of the dollar but would moderate the depreciation and greatly reduce the risk of a dollar crisis.

While the existence of a global savings glut can help explain why the large U.S. trade deficit has been sustained with relative ease well beyond what many experts had expected, it does not avoid the looming reality of there being an upper-bound on U.S. net external debt. And, that this debt ceiling creates the inevitable need for a large real depreciation of the U.S. dollar. A saving glut can explain why global real interest rates are low. But it does not avoid the problem posed by those rates being as low as rates in both the United States, a deficit country, and the surplus economies.

This anomaly occurs because foreign investors in dollar assets are not taking into account the impending need for a sustained and substantial real depreciation of the dollar. When this risk becomes apparent to those investors, they will hurry to find other destinations for their savings. If that happens, the dollar would plummet.

Bretton Woods II

Some economists have characterized the current global monetary arrangement as Bretton Woods II (BWII).[10] The first Bretton Woods (BWI) was the global monetary arrangement in place from the end of World War II through 1973. BWI was a formal system of fixed exchange rates centered on the dollar. Other countries were obliged to maintain their currencies value relative to the dollar. When needed, this adjustment was accomplished by foreign central banks buying or selling foreign exchange to keep their currencies' value at the fixed parity with the dollar. The speculative crises caused by relatively free flowing international capital that plagued the inter-war years were to be prevented by strict controls on the flow of capital between economies. This system worked reasonably well in the early post-war period. But accumulating pressure for a major dollar devaluation and increasingly porous capital controls led to its breakdown in the early 1970s. Since 1973, most major economies have allowed their currencies to, more or less, float freely on the global foreign exchange markets, allowing its exchange value to be driven by the international supply and demand for its goods and assets. Capital controls were also largely abandoned by these nations.

BWII is not a formal arrangement or organization. It is a de facto arrangement whereby central banks, particularly in Asia, amass dollar reserves so as to stabilize their currencies value relative to the dollar. This stabilization is achieved by the central banks buying dollar assets sufficient to keep their currencies from rising relative to the dollar. It is also supported by the BWII economies imposing significant controls on capital flows to and from their economies. Not letting their currencies rise relative to the dollar enables them to maintain the competitiveness of their exports in the U.S. market and perpetuate a successful development strategy driven by export-led growth. China has been a important participant in this arrangement, with its central bank in recent years amassing well over $1 trillion in foreign exchange reserves, a large proportion being various dollar assets.

With China at its center, it could be argued that because BWII has been a very successful development strategy for China, and because that country still has over 300 million non industrial workers to absorb into its industrial and service sectors, this de facto monetary arrangement will endure for many more years, and continue to exert strong upward pressure on the value of the dollar, countering any tendency towards a dollar crisis.

However, serious questions can be raised about the stability of BWII.[11] One potential problem is that such large scale accumulations of foreign exchange reserves can have disruptive macroeconomic and financial effects on the accumulating economy. To prevent the foreign exchange reserves from causing an unwanted increase the country's money supply, its central bank must *sterilize* the accumulation of foreign currency assets. It does this by purchasing compensating amounts of domestic assets which pulls money out of the economy.

Sterilization of dollar inflows on such a large and growing scale, however, will be an increasingly difficult task for China and other emerging economies. They have small and immature asset markets that are unlikely to be able to continue to effectively sterilize further large scale reserve growth. It is likely that this foreign liquidity will begin to leak into their domestic economy and push up the money supply. This would, in turn, lead to increased inflation and a domestic lending boom that generates asset price bubbles. This could cause significant disruptions in their weak financial markets and adversely affect their economic activity.

In addition, the balance sheets of the foreign central banks that hold large amounts of dollar assets are exposed to large losses if the dollar crashes. Collectively, the BWII central banks have an incentive to hold on to their dollar assets to preserve the value of these holdings. Individually, however, the BWII central banks have an incentive to sell their dollar assets if they suspect the dollar will soon plunge. Therefore, the stability of BWII is highly dependent on how much cooperation there is among these central banks.

Further, a large share of the capital inflow to the United States comes from private investors whose economic incentives are different than those of the BWII central banks. Perhaps foreign private investors remain heavily in dollar assets because they think that BWII can prevent a dollar crash. But there is no strong basis for such a belief. The efficacy of BWII would be evident if at some point it had demonstrated an ability to sustain the dollar's value despite an outflow from the United States of private capital motivated by realistic expectations about the dollar's future falling path. But, what has been occurring are large official inflows along with large private inflows that are accepting a real return that is insufficient to compensate for the expected rate of fall of the dollar which realistically must occur.

If BWII is to offset the outflow of private capital based on realistic expectations of the dollar's future path, the BWII central banks would need to increase their already huge dollar reserves by an amount that is probably not feasible. And the problem posed by there being an upper bound to the U.S. debt/GNP ratio would still remain. BWII seems unlikely to be seen as a reliable barrier to a plummeting dollar once foreign investors see the need to adjust to more realistic expectations of the dollar's future path.

Dark Matter

Another perspective on the U.S. international balances has been presented by the economists Ricardo Hausmann and Frederico Struzeneggar.[12] It is their contention that there are large measurement errors in the U.S. trade data that cause a big understatement of U.S. exports and, in turn, a big overstatement of the size of U.S. net external debt. In their opinion this error is of a magnitude that the current account balance has actually been in surplus in recent years and that the United States is an external net creditor, not a debtor. The principal evidence of this is that despite a seeming huge net external debt the United States has consistently run a sizable surplus in the investment income portion of the current account.

The unmeasured exports are not picked up in the export data because they are are services hidden within U.S. capital outflows. Once abroad, these assets generate an income stream that is measured as investment income in the current account data. These invisible assets have been named *dark matter* because they, like the astronomical phenomenon, have a visible effect — generating investment income — that is caused by unseen service exports. It is contented that the dark matter effect is large. With proper accounting, it transforms a net debt position of about $2.5 trillion to a net surplus position of about $600 billion.

Three classes of invisible exports are said to exist: global liquidity services, global insurance services, and knowledge services. The three exports, in turn, are attached respectively, to three types of capital outflows: U.S. currency, U.S. sovereign debt, and U.S. foreign direct investment.

Liquidity Services

This service is derived from the U.S. currency's special status as a global source of liquidity. A large portion of the $700 billion Federal Reserve Notes in circulation are held abroad. Estimates of the share vary from a low of 30% to a high of 70%. The holding of this currency by foreigners is equivalent to an interest free and irredeemable loan to the United States with an implicit value of as much as $25 billion.

Insurance Services

It is argued that the world economy uses low-risk U.S. Treasury Securities to fill out the low-risk end of their investment portfolios. Much like a global bank, the United States can then use these proceeds to invest in higher yielding bonds from emerging economies. This amounts to the world exchanging a risky asset for a safe asset and the yield difference is the equivalent of an insurance premium the world pays the U.S. for lowering its risk.

Knowledge Services

This service is said to occur because U.S. foreign direct investment embodies a host of unmeasured assets. These services are in the form of know-how, brand recognition, expertise, and research and development. This is the form of dark matter that proponents see as the most important.

The major implication of the dark matter argument for the dollar is that because the true state of the U.S. trade position is not precarious and because the United states is not a net external debtor, there is no need for a dollar depreciation to keep the debt to GNP ratio within bounds. Foreign investors could be quite willing to hold more dollar assets despite their having little apparent yield advantage over foreign assets. The risk of a dollar crisis in this circumstance would be small.

While there is probably some merit to the dark matter argument, most economists would argue that the scale of the effect is vastly smaller than claimed by its proponents. For that reason, economic dark matter probably does little to forestall the need for a substantial correction of the U.S. trade deficit. And that correction must be set in motion by a substantial real depreciation of the dollar, beyond the depreciation that has already occurred, and that will persist for several years.

THE MACROECONOMIC EFFECTS OF A DOLLAR CRISIS

In the standard macroeconomic model, a reduction of foreign capital inflows would have no long-term effect on aggregate spending and output. A real depreciation of the dollar would encourage U.S. export sales and discourage domestic spending on imports, *increasing net exports* and shrinking the trade deficit. At the same time foreigner's reduced willingness to hold dollar assets will reduce the inflow of foreign capital, pushing down the price of U.S. securities, and pushing up U.S. interest rates. Higher interest rates would then induce a *decrease in interest sensitive spending* such as residential investment, consumer durables, and business investment. In the end, the trade deficit would be gone, the composition of U.S. spending and output would change, but there would not be any change in the total level of spending and output.

The transition to this new equilibrium of trade balances, however, may not be smooth. Some argue that there could be a very rough transition involving a sharp slowdown in economic activity or a recession. Substantial near-term slowing of economic activity would occur if the decrease of U.S. domestic spending occurs more quickly then the increase of U.S. net-exports. Interest sensitive purchases tend to be more postponable then other domestic spending and would likely fall relatively quickly as interest rates spiked. Net exports' response could be significantly slower. The peak effect on net exports in response to a currency depreciation is usually about two years later. However, in this situation the scale of adjustment needed to eliminate the trade deficit is unusually large and will involve large shifts of resources into the production of tradable goods which take time. This could slow the response of net exports further.

What aggravates this situation and significantly adds to the risk of a dollar crisis triggering a recession is the U.S. economy's ongoing burden of adjusting to the housing price crisis. Falling home prices reduce household wealth, discouraging household spending, and dampen aggregate spending. As with most markets, there is a self correcting mechanism that facilitates beneficial adjustment in the housing market. This occurs as weaker aggregate demand also weakens the demand for credit and causes interest rates to decrease. By stimulating interest sensitive spending, falling interest rates, other things equal, arrest some of the downward impulse on aggregate demand of falling housing prices.

However, if the economy must also endure the disruptive effects of a plummeting dollar, other things would not be equal. In a dollar crisis, great numbers of foreign investors are attempting to sell large amounts of dollar assets at the same time causing dollar asset prices to fall sharply and interest rates to rise sharply. Interest rates will continue to rise until a sufficient number of dollar-averse investors can be enticed to offer enough capital to finance the slowly shrinking current account deficit. An interest rate spike like this is likely to forestall any ameliorating effect of otherwise falling interest rates on the housing crisis, slowing aggregate demand more than would otherwise occur.

In this environment, where two crises exert downward pressure on aggregate spending, the risk rises that the short-term adjustment of the U.S. trade balance could involve a much quicker and much larger slowing of domestic spending with so little near-term boost from rising net exports. This magnified near-term negative impact could be sufficient to cause a recession.

The Response of Economic Policy

The ability of conventional fiscal and monetary policy, here and abroad, to counter the near-term contractionary effects of a dollar crisis is problematic.

Response of U.S. Economic Policy

When the government budget is in deficit, it reduces domestic saving and when in surplus it increases domestic saving. Therefore, conceptually an infusion of government saving caused by policy actions that reduce the federal budget deficit could compensate for the dwindling flow of foreign savings stemming from foreign investors move out of dollar assets. Governments adding to the domestic flow of saving would tend to decrease interest rates and stimulate aggregate spending. This would also mean that the trade balance adjustment could occur with out a reduction of domestic investment. An outcome, that bodes better for productivity and the long-term growth of the U.S. living standard.

However, to get to this point there would first be an initial dampening effect flowing from the government's budget deficit reducing actions of spending less, taxing more, or doing both. In the short run, a negative fiscal impulse in conjunction with the already occurring short-run negative effects of the housing crisis and dollar crisis would amplify the recession risk. Also, the impulse toward lower interest rates would mute the self-correcting effect of a rising interest differential between dollar assets and foreign assets that would otherwise help to slow the dollar's fall.

Again, conceptually the short-term negative effects of fiscal tightening on aggregate spending could be countered by a complementary short-term monetary stimulus which spurs spending through exerting downward pressure on interest rates. In practice, however, whether alone or in tandem with monetary policy, the use of budget deficit reduction as a policy response to the near-term problems of a dollar crisis is improbable. The necessary tax and spending changes are unlikely to be implemented quickly enough. Over a longer time horizon, where fiscal action may be more likely, increased government saving from budget deficit reduction would prevent the dwindling inflows of foreign saving from causing an undesired compression of U.S. domestic investment.

With fiscal policy most likely out of consideration in the near-term, the task of attempting to counter the short-term contractionary effects of a dollar crisis would fall upon the Federal Reserve. It would most likely do this by pumping liquidity into the economy and exerting downward pressure on interest rates. Monetary policy can be implemented quickly and its favorable effect felt with a modest time lag. Nevertheless, there are some potential constraints on the Fed's ability to follow a stimulative monetary policy during a dollar crisis.

One potential constraint is a consequence of the dollar depreciation inducing a increase in U.S. inflation by causing the price of U.S. imports' to rise sharply. This inflation effect will be muted by import's relatively small share of final demand. Also many foreign producers will, to preserve market share, prevent a full pass-through of the exchange rate change to the price of their products exported to the United States. Nevertheless it is still possible that the scale of dollar depreciation in a crisis could lead to a 1 to 2 percentage point jump in the inflation rate. This inflation effect would stop once the dollar stabilized. But to prevent this inflation spurt from generating an increase in inflation expectations and causing a more enduring run-up of inflation, the Fed might be reluctant to validate those expectations by continuing to provide monetary stimulus.

Another possible constraint on fully pursuing policy of monetary stimulus is that if the fall of the dollar is seen by the Fed to be too extreme, policy action may be needed to gain some control over the falling currency. Most likely this would involve changing direction and increasing interest rates to entice foreign investors back to dollar assets.

Even if the Fed does not relent in applying monetary stimulus, the traditional channel for doing this is by targeting short-term interest rates, usually the nominal federal funds rate. However, that rate can only be decreased to zero. With the nominal federal funds rate already down to about 4.25%, there is a question of whether sufficient monetary stimulus could be applied before this rate reaches the so-called zero bound.

At this point, there are non traditional ways that might be used to implement monetary policy. These include targeting longer-termed federal securities, making direct loans to banks, or altering inflation expectations (i.e., lowering real rates via a credible commitment to higher future inflation) that could be used. It is still uncertain, however, if these untried alternative monetary policy levers are effective and, if effective, whether that effect can be delivered to the economy quickly enough to counter the sharp short-term negative impulse to domestic spending of a fast falling dollar.

Response of Foreign Economic Policy

The economic policy response of other economies, particularly those with trade surpluses, could help or hinder the macroeconomic adjustment forced by a dollar crisis. As discussed earlier, a falling dollar (and rising foreign currencies) is the instrument that will lead to a rebalancing of world spending. For economies with trade surpluses the rebalancing would manifest as a increase of domestic spending and decrease of net exports.

As was true for the United States, after the rebalancing has been completed, affected foreign economies total spending and level of output would be unchanged. The negative effects from the decrease in net-exports caused by their currencies appreciation will be counter-balanced by the positive effect from lower interest rates, pushed down by increased capital inflows, boosting domestic spending. Like the United States, however, the rest of the world's near-term transition to this new equilibrium might not be smooth, and also carry an elevated risk of recession.

Many U.S. trading partners have relied on export sales to the American market as their principal, or at least their major, engine of economic growth. This practice is most overt in those economies that tie their currency to the dollar so that dollar depreciation does not reduce the price competitiveness of their exports. In a dollar crisis, there could be a temptation to try to continue to prevent their currencies from appreciating against the dollar. Defending their currencies would slow the global adjustment. But it is unlikely to be successful policy, however, in the face of a global attempt to move out of dollar assets and a plummeting dollar. The likely aftermath of such an attempt would be that these economies would be left holding an even larger stock of dollar assets whose value is a fraction of what it was when purchased.

The deflationary impact of a rising currency would help economies, such as China, that are facing an inflation problem. On the other hand, it could cause problems for a country like Japan that still teeters on the edge of deflation.

In general, a more useful policy response by foreign economies would likely be expansionary economic policies sufficient to boost domestic spending and offset the near-term negative impact of an appreciating currency on their net exports. Because this stimulus must be applied quickly for it to be effective, the task would most likely be undertaken by the monetary authorities.

As was true for the United States, it is problematic whether the application of a stimulative monetary policy by the central banks of the surplus economies would have sufficient positive effect on aggregate spending in the near-term to avoid a strong downward push on global economic activity. In economies that are already facing a significant inflation problem, such as China, there could be a reluctance to fan the inflationary flames any further by undertaking added monetary expansion. In any event, a cooperative policy response by the United States and its major trading partners would certainly help to smooth the global adjustment to a dollar crisis.

Conclusion

Predicting the path of exchange rates is always an endeavor with an above normal level of uncertainty. Nevertheless, it seems undeniable that a further sizable depreciation of the dollar is necessary in the long run to keep the United States' large and growing external debt within realistic bounds. It is difficult, however, to predict how global investors who hold the U.S. external debt will respond to the seemingly large erosion of the value of those dollar assets caused by this inevitable depreciation of the dollar.

A rational response to holding a currency unable to perform its role as a store of value would be to move quickly into assets denominated in other more stable currencies. Yet, despite the sizable depreciation of the dollar that has already occurred, foreign investors continue to hold dollar assets. There are reasons, in addition to the store of value function, to hold those assets. Safety and liquidity are two other important reasons, both functions that the wide and deep dollar asset markets perform very well. Also, many investors pursue very long term goals and could be willing to ignore short run risk. It seems unlikely, however, that these other reasons for holding dollar assets, would continue to trump the dollar's rapidly dwindling ability to provide the store of value function. If so, then a sharp dollar fall could be just ahead.

A plummeting dollar would have positive and negative effects on the world economy as well. Eventually the positive and negative impacts on the level of economic activity should be offsetting, but it would leave the world economy with more stable external balances. But, there is reason to be concerned that in the short-run the negative effects may be dominant, raising the risk of recession.

The triggering of a recession by a plummeting dollar will depend on what else is going on in the economy when the currency crashes. If already weakened by other forces, the risk of recession would grow much larger. If generally good economic conditions prevail, then economic activity is likely to slow in the near-term but avoid a recession.

It is important to take into consideration that the U.S. economy is large and resilient, and able to absorb substantial shocks without necessarily transmitting a significant adverse effect on overall economic activity. In contrast, a dollar crisis is likely to send a more devastating economic blow to economies that are highly dependent on exporting to the U.S. market to sustain their economic growth.

REFERENCES

[1] The trade-weighted exchange rate index used is the *real broad index* reported monthly by the Board of Governors of the Federal Reserve System.

[2] For an early treatment of the dollar crisis scenario, see Stephen Marris, *Deficits and The Dollar: World Economy at Risk*, Institute for International Economics, Washington DC, 1985.

[3] For a more extensive discussion of international asset flows and the trade deficit, see CRS Report RL3 1032, *The U.S. Trade Deficit : Causes, Consequences, and Cures*, by Craig K. Elwell.

[4] Paul Krugman, "Will There Be a Dollar Crisis," *Economic Policy*, July 2007.

[5] See, for example, Micheal Obstfeld and Kenneth Rogoff, "Global Current Account Imbalances and Exchange Rate Adjustment," *Brookings Papers on Economic Activity*, no. 1, 2005.

[6] Paul Krugman, "Will There Be a Dollar Crisis," *Economic Policy*, July 2007, also examines these arguments.

[7] Most countries are not able to borrow in their own currency so a fall of their exchange rate will tend to increase their net external debt. This was the problem that plagued the economies caught in the Asian financial crisis in 1997, when their crashing currencies ballooned their external debt to such a degree that they became insolvent.

[8] For further details on net external debt and valuation effects see U.S. Department of Commerce, Bureau of Economic Analysis, *U.S. Net International Investment Position*, July 2007.

[9] See Ben Bernanke, "The Global Savings Glut and the U.S. Current Account Deficit," the Sandbridge Lecture, Virginia Association of Economics, March 10, 2005; and CRS Report RL33 140, *Is the U.S. Trade Deficit Caused by a Global Saving Glut*, by Marc Labonte.

[10] Michael P. Dooley, David Folkerts-Landau, and Peter Garber, *An Essay on the Revived Bretton Woods System*, NBER Working Paper 9971, 2003.

[11] Neil Roubini and Brad Sester, "Will the Bretton Woods II Regime Unravel Soon? The Risk of a Hard-Landing in 2005-2006," presented at Symposium sponsored by the Federal Reserve Bank of San Francisco and the University of California, Berkeley, San Francisco, 2005.

[12] Ricardo Hausmann and Federico Sturzenegger, "U.S. and Global Imbalances: Can Dark Matter Prevent the Big Bang?," (Kennedy School of Government, Harvard University, Unpublished Working Paper: Cambridge, 2005) and CRS Report RL33570, *U.S. External Debt: How Has the United Sates Borrowed Without Cost*, by Craig K. Elwell

In: Monetary Policy at the Cutting Edge
Editor: Sarah R. Porter, pp. 99-106
ISBN: 978-1-60692-321-4

Chapter 5

STRUCTURE AND FUNCTIONS OF THE FEDERAL RESERVE SYSTEM*

Pauline Smale

ABSTRACT

In 1913, Congress created the Federal Reserve System to serve as the central bank for the United States. The Federal Reserve formulates the nation's monetary policy, supervises and regulates banks, and provides a variety of financial services to depository financial institutions and the federal government. The System comprises three major components, the Board of Governors, a network of 12 Federal Reserve Banks, and member banks.

Congress created the Federal Reserve as an independent agency to enable the central bank to carry out its responsibilities protected from excessive political and private pressures. At the same time, by law and practice, the Federal Reserve is accountable to Congress. The seven members of the board are appointed by the President with the advice and consent of the Senate. Congress routinely monitors the Federal Reserve System through formal and informal oversight activities. This chapter examines the structure and operations of the major components of the Federal Reserve System, and provides an overview of congressional oversight activities.

---

* Excerpted from CRS Report RS20826, dated June 15, 2005.

Background

The U.S. central banking system was established in 1913 by the Federal Reserve Act (P.L. 63-43). Congress created the Federal Reserve (popularly known as the "Fed") as an independent entity to attend to the nation's credit and monetary needs without undue influence from political pressures. Today, the Fed's monetary policy operations are intended to promote stability in the nation's economy; its supervisory and regulatory functions are intended to provide a safer, more flexible banking system; and its work as fiscal agent for the government and clearinghouse for private sector financial transactions promotes efficiency in the overall banking system. In keeping with its independence within the federal government, the System operates without appropriations from Congress. Its income derives primarily from interest on government securities acquired through monetary policy operations, and fees for banking services, with any excess income returned to the Treasury.

The current structure of the System has three major components established by the original act. First, a Board of Governors oversees the whole System and has responsibility for monetary policy. Second, there are 12 regional Federal Reserve Banks, which carry out supervision and examination of commercial banks that are Fed members. The member banks, all national banks and all state-chartered banks that choose to be members of the System, make up the third component.

Board of Governors

The Board of Governors of the Federal Reserve System was established as a federal government agency. The Administration and Congress can have a significant influence on the Fed through control over appointments to the seven-member board. Each of the seven governors is appointed by the President, with the advice and consent of the Senate. The full term of service for a board seat is 14 years and governors may be named to a seat at any point during the term. The appointments are staggered with one term expiring every two years. Governors serving a full term may not be reappointed. Two members hold the leadership positions of chairman and vice chairman of the board. They are designated by the President, with the advice and consent of the Senate. The term of service for both leadership offices is four years; an office holder may be reappointed. These terms do not coincide with that of the President or each other. While the board chairman is considered quite powerful, each governor has one vote on the board.

When selecting a governor, the President must give due regard to a fair representation of financial, agricultural, industrial, and commercial interests, and geographical divisions of the country. No more than one governor can be selected from any one Federal Reserve district. The members of the Board of Governors cannot hold any office, position, or employment in any member bank during the time they are in office and for two years after.

Currently, all seven positions are filled but three spots will open over the next eight months. The board chairman is Alan Greenspan; he will not complete his current term as chairman because his term as governor expires in 2006. Governor Ben S. Bernanke has been nominated to be the next chairman of the White House Council of Economic Advisors and will remain at the Federal Reserve until confirmed. Governor Bernanke is serving a term that ends in 2018. Governor Edward M. Gramlich has announced that he will resign at the end of August 2005, he is serving in a term that ends in 2008. The vice chairman is Roger W. Ferguson, whose term as vice chairman expires in 2007 and whose term as governor ends in 2014. Governor Mark W. Olson is serving in a term that ends in 2010. Governor Susan Schmidt Bies is serving a full term that ends in 2012. Governor Donald L. Kohn is serving a full term that ends in 2016.

Monetary Policy

The primary responsibility of the Board of Governors of the Federal Reserve System is the formulation of monetary policy. In broad terms, monetary policy involves increasing and decreasing the supply of money and, therefore, interest rates to achieve macroeconomic objectives. The Federal Reserve uses economic instruments to alter the availability and cost of money and credit. In general, the long-term goal of monetary policy is to ensure that money and credit grow sufficiently to encourage non-inflationary economic expansion. When economic problems arise, such as the prospect of an economic downturn, attention can quickly focus on the Fed's policy decisions.[1]

The Federal Open Market Committee (FOMC) is the policy making body for open market operations — the principal means through which monetary policy is conducted. The seven board members plus five of the 12 Federal Reserve Bank presidents make up the FOMC. The president of the Federal Reserve Bank of New York is a permanent member because the New York Bank executes the Fed's monetary policy decisions through open market operations. The remaining four seats are filled by the other 11 presidents on a rotating basis for one-year terms. All of the presidents participate in the FOMC meetings and contribute their views but only the five members vote. The committee elects a chairman and vice chairman. Traditionally, the chairman of the Board of Governors is elected chairman and the New York Bank's president is elected vice chairman.

Open market operations involve the purchase and sale of government securities in the secondary market by the Federal Reserve. Payments for purchases of securities by the Federal Reserve increase the money supply and this tends to ease credit conditions. When securities are sold by the Federal Reserve the money supply is decreased and credit conditions are tightened. The Federal Reserve System's portfolio is composed of U.S. Treasury securities, federal agency securities, and bankers acceptances. The Federal Reserve Bank of New York holds the portfolio and through its trading desk conducts open market operations pursuant to directives of the FOMC.

Two less often used monetary policy instruments may be employed by the Federal Reserve — legal reserve requirements and the discount window. Depository financial institutions are required by law to set aside reserves in certain proportions against demand deposits. What is held in reserve affects the availability of loanable funds. An increase in the requirement would mean banks and thrifts would have less money to lend and would tend to restrain the money supply. Alternatively, lowering the requirement would increase the proportion of deposits that could be lent and would tend to expand the money supply. Reserve requirements are rarely changed because as a monetary policy tool they are considered too blunt an instrument.

The discount window is the Federal Reserve facility for lending to eligible depository institutions. An institution may borrow funds for short periods from a Federal Reserve Bank to augment its reserve balances for interbank transactions. The discount rate is the interest rate charged for this short-term loan. The rate is set by each Bank subject to approval by the Board of Governors; over time, it has become common practice for the rate to be uniform for all 12 Reserve Banks. A higher rate discourages borrowing and in turn lending by banks and thrifts. The operations of the discount window are not as efficient as open market operations. Currently, the discount window serves mainly as a complement to open market operations.

Supervision and Regulation

The Board of Governors has a broad range of supervisory and regulatory responsibilities that affect the entire U.S. banking system. The board seeks to promote safety and soundness, ensure compliance with laws and regulation, and foster the fair and efficient delivery of services to customers of financial institutions.

Federal Reserve Board regulations implement policies set by Congress that are defined in legislation and referred to the Federal Reserve for enforcement. For example, the Fed has implementation and enforcement responsibilities for the Truth in Lending Act, the Electronic Funds Transfer Act, and the Fair Housing Act. The board coordinates its activities with other federal and state regulatory agencies. The board has the power to examine all member banks and their affiliates and to require periodic reports from them.

The board has the primary responsibility for supervising and regulating bank holding companies and state-chartered banks that are members of the Federal Reserve System. In addition, the board supervises corporations through which U.S. banks conduct operations abroad, and the U.S. operations of foreign banks. The board delegates many supervisory duties to the 12 Reserve Banks subject to the board's policy and oversight. An example is the task of conducting bank examinations.

The Board of Governors has broad oversight and supervisory authority over the operations and activities of the Federal Reserve Banks. The board appoints three of the nine directors of each Bank. The Board conducts annual financial examinations of the Reserve Banks. Major expenditures, such as building construction, must be approved by the board. The salaries of Reserve Bank presidents and first vice presidents are subject to board approval.

Federal Reserve Banks

The 12 Federal Reserve Banks carry out the day-to-day operations of the Federal Reserve System. Within each geographic district a city was designated as the location of the Reserve Bank. The act also provided for branch offices to support the operations of the Federal Reserve Banks. The 12 Banks are located in Boston, New York, Philadelphia, Cleveland, Richmond, Atlanta, Chicago, St. Louis, Minneapolis, Kansas City, Dallas, and San Francisco. The Board of Governors has established 25 branches over the years.

Each Federal Reserve Bank is managed by a nine-member board of directors that is divided into three classes: A, B, and C. They serve three-year terms on a staggered basis. The three Class A and Class B directors are elected by the member banks in each district. Three Class C directors are appointed by the Board of Governors. The three Class A directors represent the interests of the member banks. The remaining six directors represent the general public and are selected with due consideration to the interests of agriculture, commerce, industry, services, labor, and consumers. Class B and C directors cannot be officers, directors or employees of any banking institution. In addition, Class C directors cannot hold stock in a bank or bank holding company. The board designates one Class C director as chairman and another as deputy chairman. Each Reserve Bank is headed by a president appointed by the nine directors with the approval of the Board of Governors.

The District Banks are the principal medium through which the general supervisory powers of the Fed are executed. Federal Reserve Banks conduct on-site examinations of state member banks and inspections of bank holding companies and their nonbank subsidiaries.

The Federal Reserve Banks provide fiscal agency and depository services to the federal government. For example, as fiscal agents they issue, transfer, exchange and redeem government securities and savings bonds. As depositories, they provide transaction accounts for the Treasury and they collect and disburse funds on behalf of the federal government.

The 12 Reserve Banks provide banking services to depository financial institutions. The Banks maintain reserve and clearing accounts for banks and thrifts. The Banks play a major role in the nation's payment system. Reserve Banks move coin and currency into and out of circulation. They also participate in the collection and processing of millions of checks daily. The Banks are an integral part of electronic funds transfer systems, clearing and settling electronically originated credits and debits.

The income of the Federal Reserve Banks is primarily generated from interest on government securities acquired through open market operations. In addition, the Monetary Control Act of 1980 requires the Federal Reserve to charge fees for various services. From their earnings the Reserve Banks pay their operating and other expenses. The Banks are assessed semiannually by the Board of Governors for the board's costs and expenditures. The residual earnings are turned over to the U.S. Treasury. Payments to the Treasury in 2004 totaled $18.1 billion.[2]

MEMBER BANKS

The Federal Reserve Act requires all national banks to be members of the Federal Reserve System. National banks are banks chartered by the federal government. Membership by state-chartered banks is optional. If state-chartered banks elect to become members they must meet the standards set by the Board of Governors. As of June 30, 2004, there were 1,955 national banks and 930 state-chartered Federal Reserve member banks. While these banks represented only about 38% of all federally insured U.S. banks, they held about 79% of all insured bank assets.[3] The 12 Reserve Banks are "owned" by their member banks. The stock of the Federal Reserve Banks is held entirely by the member banks in their respective districts. Ownership of this stock does not carry the usual rights of control and financial interest ordinarily associated with being a shareholder in a corporation operated for the purpose of making a profit. Each member bank buys stock in its district Reserve Bank equal to 6% of its own capital and surplus. Of this amount, 3% must be paid-in and 3% is subject to call by the Board of Governors. The stock may not be sold or pledged as security for loans. Dividends are set by law at the rate of 6% per year on paid-in stock.

Congressional Oversight

Throughout the history of the Federal Reserve System, Congress has been concerned with achieving a balance between assuring independence for the System's operations and making the agency accountable for its actions. Attention to Federal Reserve accountability has resulted in increased disclosure by the Fed and dialogue between the Fed and Congress on monetary policy and the agency's operations overall. Avenues of communication and oversight, both formal and informal, have developed over time.

Aside from its appointment role, Congress exercises oversight in a variety of ways. The Federal Banking Agency Audit Act (P.L. 95-320) was enacted in 1978 to enhance congressional oversight responsibilities. The law gave the General Accounting Office (GAO; now the Government Accountability Office) the authority to audit the Board of Governors, the Reserve Banks and branches. Such audits are limited, however, as GAO is prohibited from auditing monetary policy operations, foreign transactions, and the FOMC operations. Congressional oversight on these matters is exercised through the requirement for reports and through semi-annual monetary policy hearings.

Reports and Hearings

The Federal Reserve publishes numerous reports during the year which are important to the oversight work of Congress. The Board of Governors publishes an annual report of activities which includes the minutes of the FOMC meetings. The board is required by law to report annually on compliance with its consumer regulations. The Federal Reserve issues reports and surveys on a variety of subjects, for example an annual survey of bank fees and services and a report on the profitability of credit card operations.

The Fed is frequently called upon to testify on a wide range of issues affecting the economy and the banking industry. In addition, a monetary policy reporting system, accomplished through hearings, was made a matter of legislative mandate in the Federal Reserve Reform Act of 1977 (P.L. 95-188). The process was modified by provisions embodied in P.L. 95-523, the Humphrey-Hawkins Act of 1978. The provisions are designed to enhance the dialogue on monetary policy between Congress and the Federal Reserve through a more detailed reporting and evaluation process than existed earlier. Further, the provisions are intended to contribute to the ability of Congress to take a coordinated look at government economic policies. The two goals are sought through a system of regularly scheduled oversight hearings at which the Federal Reserve reports to the banking committees on its policy intention. The banking committees in turn report to their respective houses.

The statutory requirements for semi-annual monetary policy reporting, the board's annual report and several other reports would have been discontinued by provisions of the 1995 Federal Reports Elimination and Sunset Act (P.L. 104-66). Provisions contained in P.L. 106-569, enacted on December 27, 2000, reinstated these requirements.

REFERENCES

[1] For more information on monetary policy, see CRS Report RL30354, *Monetary Policy: Current Policy and Conditions,* by Gail Makinen and Marc Labonte.

[2] U.S. Federal Reserve System, 2004 Annual Report of the Board of Governors of the Federal Reserve System, April 2005, p.129.

[3] Ibid. p.289.

INDEX

C

D

E

H

I

J

L

M

N

O

P

R

S

T

U

V

W

Y